TAKE BACK CONTROL OF YOUR MIND

A Guide to Understanding, Taming, and Controlling
Your Thoughts and Emotions, and Thereby
Achieving True Happiness and Inner Peace

GLENN N. LEVINE, MD, FACC, FAHA

Master Clinician and Professor of Medicine, Baylor College of Medicine
Chief, Cardiology Section, Michael E. DeBakey
VA Medical Center Houston TX

Serenity
Now
Press

ISBN 978-1-7348720-0-2
Library of Congress Control Number: 2020907738

Serenity
Now
Press

To Lydia, who started me on this transformative journey, and who most inspires me to try to become and be a better person.

CONTENTS

ACKNOWLEDGMENTS

I give humble thanks and gratitude to the many authors, teachers, lecturers, instructors, and spiritual leaders who have helped illuminate and inspire me. My deepest appreciation to Paula Fitzgerald for her outstanding editing, Ryan Biore for his design of the book cover, to Lydia May for her artistic direction, and to David Wogahn and his team for all their work to bring this book to fruition.

Namaste.

PREFACE

I t was not until I was in my fifties that I finally began to understand, as radical and counterintuitive as it may at first sound, that I did not control my mind. This revelation began almost a decade ago, when I went for the first time on a weeklong cruise with my wife-to-be Lydia. I had never been a sit-on-a-boat, stare-into-space type person, but she made me an offer I could not refuse: if I went on the cruise, she would pay for it. So off we went. I decided to go all in. I went completely off the grid: no computer, no email, no texting, no internet—not even ESPN. For the first time in my busy, hard-charging, frenetic life, my mind was completely calm. No worries, no planning, no anxieties, no frustrations, no endless thoughts of the past, no concerns about the future. I saw what a mind at peace could be like. And it was wonderful!

While on the cruise, I read an amazing book called *Don't Sweat the Small Stuff . . . and It's All Small Stuff* by Richard Carlson. This book led me to begin to understand how we overreact to the daily events of life and allow such events to cause us undo and pointless anxiety, remorse, worry, and stress. I next read a book Lydia had bought me called *The Buddha Walks into a Bar* by Lodro Rinzler. Lydia was thinking the "bar" in the title might suck me into actually reading it. The book presented a secular, scientifically sound paradigm of how we allow our thoughts, emotions, worries, desires, and aversions to perturb our natural state of happiness; how these thoughts lead to discontentment and dissatisfaction with our present lives and contribute to feelings of sadness, regret, and suffering; and how we allow our minds to adversely influence our behavior toward others and ourselves.

I was hooked by these concepts, insights, and revelations. Now, at the time, I was a pretty happy and successful person with probably no more or no less anxiety and stress in my life than most people; I was not looking to "find myself" or embark upon some "spiritual journey." And although I considered myself a pretty good human being, I nonetheless saw an intriguing pathway toward greater happiness and inner peace, and a road map to being a better person.

So I decided to plunge in deeper. I took up meditation, went to a few meditation retreats, read dozens of books on mindfulness, meditation and Eastern philosophies, and listened to innumerable talks and podcasts on these topics. I began to explore my own mind and to contemplate how and why I reacted to people, situations, and events the way I did; why I could not keep myself from replaying unpleasant past memories or frustrating interactions with people; why I could not stop myself from thinking about upcoming events, meetings, and obligations; the causes of my apprehension and anxiety; and how I could be a better person to my loved ones.

PREFACE

I began to recognize that it is not the endless occurrences, incidents, and personal interactions of daily life that determine our mood and mental state, but rather how we react, or choose to react, to such occurrences. I started to comprehend how we allow the slightest annoyance, unexpected event, or disagreement to affect our frame of mind and disrupt our fragile state of tranquility. I started to think about abstract and esoteric concepts such as true happiness and inner peace. I began to realize that though we all desire to be happy, we do not understand what leads to true happiness, and we undermine our happiness with constant yearnings and cravings for things to be different, for things to be better, to have what we do not have and to have more of what we already have. I began to discern that happiness is determined not by external factors, but by our attitude toward and appreciation for what we already have, and that we already have more than enough to be happy right here, right now.

I realized that instead of living blissfully in the present, we pointlessly squander our days flagellating ourselves with unpleasant memories of the past and concerns about the future. We wait for the weekend, the next vacation, or even until retirement to begin enjoying our lives, when the truth is we can enjoy our lives right now. We sleepwalk through life, and only on our deathbed do we realize that we would have lived our lives differently had we known better.

These years of meditation, contemplation, reading, and learning led to invaluable insights. Though for most of my life I had believed that I controlled my own thoughts, emotions, reactions, and actions, probably like you do as well, I came to understand this was not so. Most of the time, my mind was on autopilot or, worse yet, was endlessly hijacked by what I call our subconscious *subminds*, such as our worry submind, anxiety submind, frustration submind, envy submind, insecurity submind, hedonism submind, machismo submind, and craving submind. Amazingly, we think an estimated 60,000 thoughts a day. And most of our thoughts we would not consciously choose to think. We do not choose what we think, but rather our subconscious subminds do.

In short, I realized that the vast majority of us, myself included, do not control our own minds. In order for us to take control of our lives, we must first learn to take back control of our minds. The good news is that there is a pathway forward to accomplishing this goal. Once we learn to recognize these detrimental thoughts and emotions, generated by our subconscious subminds, we can then mitigate, tame, control, and ultimately eliminate (or at least minimize) them, allowing us to restore our natural state of inner peace.

We can develop *mindfulness*—an awareness of what our mind is thinking and feeling in the present moment. Mindfulness is the most powerful of tools for dealing with the endless events of life that come at us every day, such as unpleasant interpersonal interactions, hurtful speech, personal disappointments, and the inevitable occurrences and challenges at work and at home. Mindfulness is our means toward establishing equanimity—a calm and balanced mental state of mind—that allows us to live in the now and to ultimately become a better person.

We can learn how not to sleepwalk through life. We can learn not to postpone our happiness until some ill-defined time in the future, but instead to live in the now, where there is more than enough to be happy. The more I began to incorporate these concepts, insights, and strategies into my own life, and the more I developed this thing called mindfulness, the better I became at recognizing when I was not controlling my mind; the less I would flagellate myself about the past or worry about the future; and the more I would appreciate all that I have right now. I experienced what I would now describe as an extremely pleasant feeling of *inner peace*.

I even—seemingly—became a better person. Several years into my transformative journey, my then 80-year-old mother observed, during a family vacation, that I was a lot calmer and kinder than in the past. This backhanded compliment was her way of telling me something along the lines of "You're a much better person than you used to be."

I tell you this because I believe that just as I have experienced this wonderful transformation of better appreciating life, relaxing more, worrying less, and treating people better, you can too.

When I started this journey, I was not someone particularly interested in philosophy or psychology, who sat on a mountain top and pondered the stars, the mind, or our existential existence. Rather, I was a hard-working, results driven, middle class, nine to five, red-blooded, Western-thinking, apple pie American who, after work, prefered jeans and overly worn tee shirts, and on weekends sucked down a cold beverage or two. If I, with my science oriented, data-driven, Spock-like logical, type "A" personality brain can buy into and incorporate into my life this Eastern philosophy, self-help mindfulness stuff, so can you.

My motivation for writing this modest little book is to share with you some of the lessons I have learned and insights I have had that have allowed me to be a little bit happier; to have a greater appreciation for life; to have fewer, and shorter lived, negative emotions and thoughts; to be a little more caring and a better person toward others; and to have a greater degree of inner peace. It is my hope that my story inspires you, if even just a little bit, to begin a journey down this path of understanding and ultimately better controlling your mind, and to perhaps be happier, have a little more inner peace, and become at least a little better person to not only others, but to yourself as well.

Charles Swindoll, a twentieth-century Christian pastor, famously observed that "Life is 10% what happens to you, and 90% how you react to it." This book is about the ninety percent.

In this book, we will discuss how you do not control your mind, but can learn to do so. How you can learn to better recognize when you start to think negative or detrimental thoughts or have undesirable emotions and how to mitigate them. How you can more consistently *respond* to people, events, and circumstances in a thoughtful manner, rather than *react* thoughtlessly and primitively to them. How you can use meditation to better understand your mind and to develop mindfulness. How you can understand how to deal with the endless challenges of everyday life, big and small. And how you can start to live in the present and not sleepwalk through life.

The Dalai Lama said "Happiness is determined more by the state of our mind than by our external circumstances. Working on our mental outlook is a more effective means of achieving happiness than seeking it through external sources such as wealth, position or even physical health." When we better learn to understand and control our mind, then we can control our life, our degree of happiness, and our state of inner peace. It is an endeavor well worth embarking upon.

Many of the concepts in this book are based on my original thoughts and ideas. Many others are based on what I learned from the insights and teachings of true experts on mindfulness, meditation, neuroscience and neuropsychology, and Eastern (mostly Buddhist, but also Tao, Shinto, and Hindu) philosophies. As an academician, I have striven as best I can to acknowledge and credit others when I have discussed their teachings, thoughts, and concepts. In the appendix, you'll find books that have served as inspiration for parts of this book and that may be helpful to you. I give thanks to not only the authors of these books, but to the dozens of other authors of books that have helped illuminate and inspire me.

I have intentionally kept the size of each chapter brief, so it can be read in five to ten minutes—about the attention span of most of us these days. At the end of each chapter is a symbol called a *unalome*. It is said to be an ancient Hindu or Buddhist symbol, symbolizing one's journey from disorganized and unskillful thought, triumphing over the many twists, turns, and adversities of life, and achieving wisdom, peace, and enlightenment, as represented by the lotus flower. May the words and discussions in this book facilitate your path toward happiness and inner peace. Namaste.

TAKE BACK CONTROL OF YOUR MIND

CHAPTER 1

YOU DON'T CONTROL
YOUR MIND

You don't control your mind. I'll repeat that—you don't control your mind. For most of us, during almost all of our waking hours, the mind is on autopilot or, worse yet, hijacked and controlled not by you, but by what we will call the many subconscious minds or *subminds*, located someplace inside your skull, lurking in your brain's subconsciousness. These subminds include your insecurity submind, your envy submind, your worry submind, your machismo submind, your frustration submind, your anxiety submind, and your hedonism submind. These subminds, not you, send you into episodes of frustration, sadness, worry, anxiety, and anger. They lead you to crave things you do not need or want to avoid. They cause you to think thoughts you would not want to think, remember things you would not choose to rehash in your mind, or worry about things that may or may not happen in the future, for which you have no control over anyhow. They perturb your natural state of happiness and inner peace.

TAKE BACK CONTROL OF YOUR MIND

It is likely that upon first being challenged by the statement that you do not control your mind, you simply, or conceptually, do not, or cannot, believe this to be true, but it is so. To begin to understand this concept, let me invite you to do the following experiment. See if you can do nothing else other than pay attention to your breathing for five minutes (or even just sixty seconds), without getting distracted and your thoughts beginning to wander. See if you can focus on nothing more than the in-breath and the out-breath, without thinking thoughts of the past, concerns of the future, or allowing your mind to wander in other ways. If you truly control your mind and have decided that this is what you are going to do to prove me wrong, then this exercise should be easy. But I'll bet that before long, your mind becomes distracted by thoughts, desires, memories or worries. Please go ahead and try this . . .

Let me give you another example to help you understand this critical concept. Recall a vacation, such as a carefully planned and long-awaited trip to a beautiful tropical beach. You are there to do nothing but relax and appreciate the beauty and warmth of the beach, the refreshing ocean air, and the calming effects of the sand and water. But are you really in the moment while you are there? Do your thoughts uncontrollably wander to work and your unfair boss, to a bad distant memory of an old boyfriend, or to worries about the future? Before you know it, you have squandered the last thirty minutes of precious beach time, fixated on how that jerk boss disrespects you and doesn't appreciate how valuable you are to the business. You grow increasingly frustrated and upset. You think of going back to your room, turning on your computer or smartphone, and firing off some venomous email or text to him (or to

2

the boyfriend who dumped you, or to your annoying step-mother). If you really controlled your mind, is that what you would choose to think about while on vacation?

To paraphrase Buddhist monk Sakyong Miphan, the next time you are angry, frustrated, or sad, ask yourself: *Who decided to make me feel this way?* Certainly, if we really controlled our mind, we would not consciously choose at any time to be angry, frustrated, or sad. Would we?

What about when you vow to diet but then binge eat in response to a small frustration at work? Or when you vow to be a better, more patient parent, then snap and yell at your child for accidentally spilling her milk? Are you con-trolling your mind then?

Dr. Rick Hanson, a famous neuropsychologist and author of the books *Hardwiring Happiness* and *Buddha's Brain*, has observed:

> *Only we humans*
> *worry about the future,*

3

regret the past,
and blame ourselves for the present.

If we really controlled our minds, would we choose to do any of these things he lists? The Western Buddhist teachers Joseph Goldstein and Jack Kornfield similarly note:

> *We sometimes experience great anger*
> *over past events that are long gone*
> *and about which we can do nothing.*
> *Strangely enough, we can even get*
> *furious over something that has not*
> *happened, but that we only imagine*
> *might.*

We have all fallen into this trap. Time after time after time. I, for one, would prefer not to keep getting myself frustrated or upset, wasting my time and my life thinking about the past, or fretting about the future, day after day after day, for no good reason. Yet, it is only over the past decade that I began to recognize how little I controlled my own mind. It is likely that upon a little reflection, you may reach a similar conclusion.

Do you want to be the puppet on a string, constantly having your strings pulled and manipulated by your sub-minds, endlessly having them dictate how you think, feel, and act, or do you want to take control of your mind and be the puppeteer? Only when we learn to take control of our thoughts, can we take control of our mind and our life.

In this book, we will first look at how our subminds hijack our conscious mind, and how our brains have evolved to overreact to things that, in the scheme of life, are neither truly life-threatening nor important to our survival and wellbeing. We will discuss how something called *mindfulness* can help us recognize when our mind is being hijacked, and how we can use meditation and other practices to understand how our mind works in order to seize back control of it. We will explore some easy tricks and tactics to realize when our thoughts and emotions are becoming off-kilter, and how to quickly right the ship. We will learn to better appreciate what we have right here, right now, in the present, and to not sleepwalk through life or defer our happiness to some ill-defined future, squandering away our lives. And we will review how we can use these methods to increase our happiness and reduce our suffering to achieve a greater degree of inner peace and to be a better person. In short, we will learn how to take back control of our minds.

CHAPTER 2

SUBMINDS

I f you don't control your mind most of the time, then what does? The answer, in a conceptually simplified manner, is the many subconscious minds that we will call your subminds, or what others have referred to as subbrains, subconsciousness, mind regions, mental domains, or mindstreams. You might conceptually choose to consider these subminds as your character or personality foibles, flaws, shortcomings, vices, or even demons. Or, you may think of them as the sources of the endless narratives in your head that perturb your happiness, equanimity, and inner peace.

The concept of subminds dates back hundreds and even several thousands of years and appears in one form or another in theological, philosophical, psychological, and even evolutionary writings. More recently, one concept of subminds that has garnered a great deal of interest is that which has been eloquently discussed by Dr. John Yates (a.k.a. Culadasa), a neurophysiologist and meditation master, in his wonderfully informative book *The Mind Illuminated*.

It is useful to discuss a modified concept of subminds that I have synthesized, based on the writings of John Yates and many others, Eastern and Western philosophical and psychological concepts, and years of meditation and contemplation figuring out how my own mind works. We can think of subminds as discrete parts of our subconscious that have their own functions, agendas, desires, cravings, and reactions. Examples of subminds would include your anxiety submind, anger submind, insecurity submind, hedonism submind, worry submind, envy submind, ego submind, gluttony submind, and machismo submind. Your envy submind, for example, is not content with what you have, but rather desires the wealth, fame, fortune, fancier car, bigger diamond, luxurious boat, and grandiose house of your neighbors, family, friends, or those you see on TV shows and in magazine articles. Your insecurity submind replays again and again in your head comments that others have made to you in the past, wondering what they *really* meant and what they are saying about you behind your back. Your hedonistic submind can't resist anything that

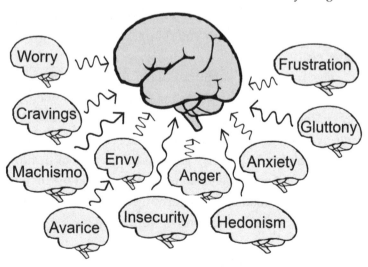

8

brings temporary pleasure and screams out for that lard-filled cupcake, five-star penthouse hotel room, heart-attack inducing double rack of ribs, and ill-advised extramarital tryst. Your ego and machismo subminds are on the constant lookout for any perceived personal slight, just waiting to erupt with indignation, anger, and outrage. Your gluttony submind just wants more, more, more.

All of these subminds have their own narrow agendas, desires, fears, emotions, aversions, and cravings. They are constantly vying for the attention of your conscious mind. When one of these subminds has a strong urge, impulse, or reaction, that thought or emotion bubbles up from your subconsciousness and takes over your conscious thought.

Remember those police radar detectors that everyone had in their cars back in the 1980s and 1990s? Whenever they detected a police radar gun aimed in the direction of your upcoming car, the radar detectors would beep incessantly louder and louder. Think of your subminds as functioning in a similar manner. Your subminds are constantly on, and whenever they detect something that sets them off, such as your ego or machismo submind detecting the smallest of perceived slights, your subminds start screaming out to your conscious mind. Only your subminds may be set to maximum sensitivity, so that ANYTHING that might fall within their domain of interest sets them off, and the mute button does not work to stop them from relentlessly alerting your mind.

For tweens and millennials, you may prefer to conceptually visualize these subminds as apps on your smartphone. Only, these apps are *always* running, and they, not you, control what appears on your phone's screen (i.e., in your mind). Further, these dozens of apps, including Twitter and

9

Instagram, have been programmed to endlessly alert you whenever anyone (e.g., any submind) sends out a message, whenever a friend makes a new post on Facebook, or whenever any website notifies you of even the slightest bit of so-called news. Every waking minute, there is another alert or notification. This is what is happening to your inundated mind.

Stimuli or events that may set off one of these subminds could include a recollection of a troubling or embarrassing memory, a flashback of an old girlfriend who dumped you, the sight of a piece of chocolate cake, a recent unpleasant interaction with someone, or concern or fear over a future event. For instance, you may be walking happily in a park, enjoying the day, when your ego or machismo submind recalls a perceived slight you suffered at the hands of your partner, neighbor, or boss. A feeling of anger builds in the submind, and this strong emotion explodes into your consciousness like a geyser spewing its boiling contents, taking control of your mind and your thoughts. You certainly would not choose to ruin your relaxing walk by replaying over and over in your mind this anger-inducing interaction, but that is exactly what happens! In fact, the more you try to forget and ignore this past incident, the more you think and perseverate about it again and again, and the more upset or angry you become, repeatedly throwing even more fuel on the fire.

Let's examine another example. You have consciously vowed to lose a few pounds and eat healthily and have been able to stick to that for a few days. As you stroll down the street though, you pass a bakery (or pizza joint, Italian restaurant, or ice cream parlor). Your hedonism or gluttony submind becomes stimulated and hyper-energized and takes over your conscious mind, leading you, contrary to your recent vows and against you better judgment, to order and gobble down a heaping piece of seven-layer cake (or pizza or rack of ribs). Since you had decided to eat healthily and lose weight, surely *you* are not controlling your mind, something else is, and that something else is your hedonism or gluttony submind.

In reality there is no single anatomic correlate in your brain for each of these subminds, although there are anatomical and evolutionary primitive parts of your brain, which we'll discuss in the next chapter, that are focused upon emotion, primitive drives, and reactions. The workings of the brain are infinitely more complex than this simple construct. Nevertheless, it is extremely helpful in your battle to take back control of your mind to be able to recognize when you are not controlling your mind, but one of these subminds is, causing you to react, succumb to an urge or impulse, or perseverate and become angered by a distant memory or possible future event, that you would not consciously choose to do.

The construct of subminds allows us to identify what is causing us to think, react, or act in a manner we would not willfully opt to do. It also allows us to de-identify with these emotions and desires, viewing them not as "me" but as an external force, emotion, or desire, allowing us to become better at keeping them at arm's length and resisting their influences upon our mind.

In the many books I have read over the last decade, it is written that our natural state is one of happiness and inner peace. While I bought into many other concepts in these books, I regarded that claim as new age gobbledygook. That is, until one day while meditating, I had a moment of insight that this really is true. When the mind is totally quiet, without worries, frustrations, concerns, anxieties, or cravings, there really is this incredible feeling of inner peace, and it is wonderful to experience. Unfortunately for us, our subminds, and their thoughts and emotions, are endlessly perturbing our inner peace.

Why was I, like so many others, skeptical and cynical about believing this is our natural state? Because throughout our teens and adult life, in our concrete jungle, high-pressure, high-stress, need-to-succeed, competitive, one-up-another, materialistic, more-more-more, email-texting-Facebook-Instagram lives, this natural state is *almost always* being disrupted by a submind—its thoughts, anxieties, desires, indignation, worries, or cravings. As a result, we have long since forgotten what a state of happiness and inner peace feels like.

I don't really blame our subminds. They do not understand or know that we, right now, have all that we need in order to have happiness and inner peace. They do not understand how they cause us emotional distress, discontent, dissatisfaction, and suffering. They do not see the big picture. They are only focused on their own narrow wants, concerns, fears, anxieties, ego, and cravings. But if we can learn to recognize and mitigate the negative vibes that emanate from our subminds, we can return to that natural state of happiness and inner peace, or at least be a little happier and experience more inner peace.

There is a hip Buddhist monk named Reverend Kusala Bhikshu, who rides a motorcycle and plays the blues on harmonica, and who during one podcast was speaking about how meditation helped him understand what happiness was. He summed up his understanding of happiness as being in the following state of mind:

Not needing it to be any better,
not fearing it will be any worse.

How cool would that be (as he is fond of saying)? In order to get there though, we must first understand and tame our subminds. Please take a minute and contemplate the many subminds you have that lead you to think and act in a manner you would not consciously choose.

CHAPTER 3

YOUR PLEISTOCENE-ERA BRAIN

Even though we live in modern times, neuropsychologists point out that our brains are still stuck in the Pleistocene era, a time period that began 2.6 million years ago and lasted until the last ice age, about 11,700 years ago. During this time, our brains evolved with the specific purposes of avoiding starvation, danger, and death, so we could survive and propagate our genes to the next generation. Our brains were designed to function in a hostile and dangerous environment in which we needed to be constantly on guard for attack by a saber-toothed tiger, to have heightened and ever present levels of fear and apprehension, and to worry about each and every snap of a twig that could signal an approaching threat to our lives. In the past, it was better to have overreacted to any perceived threat rather than be eaten alive. We had to constantly worry about the immediate future, such as where our next meal was coming from and if a tribe across the river was about to attack us. We needed to pay more attention to negative thoughts and feelings, like fear and hunger, than to positive or pleasant ones. In fact, becoming too content could lead us to drop our guard, become complacent, and perish.

Like many other animals, Pleistocene-era human males had to establish and display their machismo to impress a potential female mate and to intimidate other males away. Females had to worry about who they would mate with and the surrounding competition. Pleistocene brains evolved to make us covet our neighbor's bigger and safer cave, positioned higher up on the mountain with a better view of the terrain. Our brains evolved to be focused constantly on the immediate needs of *me, me, me*—there was no time, or reward, for thinking about the needs, desires, and preferences of others.

Our Pleistocene brains were not designed to function in our present urban, fast-paced, concrete jungle, digital rat race that is today's world. Evolution did not account for gossipy neighbors, petty coworkers, moody partners, internet haters and trolls, text messaging, Facebook, Instagram, or Twitter. Our brains have not evolved and adapted enough since the Pleistocene era to comprehend that each little occurrence in everyday life is not a threat to our existence. They have not evolved to understand that, at least in developed countries, there is generally enough to eat and drink, and shelter for most. Our brains have not lost that primitive drive of me, me, me and more, more, more. In current lingo, our brains, and minds, are functioning on a two-million-year-old computer operating system that has not been updated for modern society, so we are much like the harried and stressed-out soul on the next page.

This is the underlying cause of much of our tendency to overreact to the small stuff in life, like an unpleasant comment someone makes about us, someone cutting in front of us in line at the grocery store, or a traffic jam that makes

us a few minutes late. This is why we tend to have negative biases and emotions—worry, regret, anxiety, envy, and dissatisfaction—rather than positive emotions and feelings such as contentment, happiness, and inner peace.

Neuropsychologist Dr. Rick Hanson sums it up as follows:

> *We have evolved to pay great attention to unpleasant experiences. This negativity bias overlooks good news, highlights bad news, and creates anxiety.*

Author and teacher Ed Halliwell, a leader in the mindfulness movement, similarly notes that

> *We've evolved to tune in to the fearful more than the reassuring, to focus on problems rather than joys, with a*

bias to the unpleasant rather than the pleasant.

Does any of this sound familiar?

In simple terms, we can divide our brains into three areas: the instinctive brain; the emotional brain; and the more evolved thinking brain (the cortical "gray matter"). The instinctive brain is the most primitive part of our brain, thoughtlessly and immediately reacting to stimuli and changes in the environment.

The emotional brain includes what is referred to as the limbic system, which generates our emotions and our emotional responses. The limbic system includes the hippocampus, amygdala, hypothalamus, pituitary gland, and basal ganglia. Dr. Rick Hanson refers to the amygdala as the brains "alarm bell," responding to emotionally charged or negative stimuli. The pituitary gland triggers stress hormones. The hippocampus helps detect threats, real or imagined. And the basal ganglia seeks rewards and stimulation.

Our thinking brain, particularly the prefrontal cortex, is composed of the more evolved gray matter neurons. The prefrontal cortex can help regulate and keep in check some of our more primitive reactions, but it works slower than our more primitive mind and can take time, sometimes too much time, to do self-regulate.

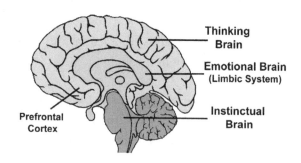

18

We can think of our subminds, such as our anger submind, our gluttony submind, and our worry submind, as residing in the more primitive instinctive and emotional (limbic system) parts of our brain. These areas of our brain quickly, even instantaneously, react to sounds, situations, and the words and actions of others. There's no gray matter filter or circuit breaker that allows one to pause and contemplate if we are overreacting or getting worked up over nothing, or the effects upon others of how we too often thoughtlessly react, or overreact, to speech or situations. These more primitive parts of our brains often think only in black and white. Something is either good or bad, friend or foe. There is no room for shades of gray. There is no room for nuance. There is no room for understanding things in context. The Dalai Lama cautions us that "black or white thinking" (such as the instantaneous decisions our subminds make) hijacks reasoning, logic, and critical thinking by largely bypassing the centers of higher thinking in the brain.

It is in the more evolved thinking brain where we can develop what is called *mindfulness*. With mindfulness, we recognize our more primitive initial responses to words, people, situations, and events, and then respond thoughtfully, rather than reacting instinctively, to these stimuli and occurrences.

Our thinking brain is a blessing, but if it is unregulated, it can also be a curse, leading us to think, remember, and obsess about unpleasant events in the past, or in the future (most of which will never even come to pass!).

While we can divide our brain into three simple areas, in reality, our brains are incredibly complex. According to Rick Hanson, a human brain weighs only three pounds, yet it contains 1.1 trillion cells, including a 100 billion neurons.

Each of these neurons receives on average 5000 connections from other neurons. And each neuron fires five to fifty times per second. By his calculations, this means that every few seconds quadrillions of signals travel inside our head. And even though our brain is only two percent of our body weight, it uses twenty to twenty-five percent of our body's oxygen and glucose requirements. This gives us some idea of how active our subminds are, and the potential for them to sow mischief, insecurity, fear, frustration, and anger in our thoughts and mind.

So how can we take back control of our mind from these Pleistocene subminds, and how can we control our thinking brain from over-revving and careening out of control like a runaway train? As we'll discuss in later chapters, we'll use our thinking brain to develop mindfulness, which will allow us to pause, think, and respond skillfully to a comment, occurrence, or situation, like a truly evolved, thoughtful, and compassionate twenty-first century human being. We'll be able to use our prefrontal cortex and thinking gray matter to learn how to recognize when a primitive submind is overreacting or luring us into an action.

We can begin to differentiate between what thoughts, things, and actions give us true happiness, and what we delude ourselves into believing will bring us happiness sometime in an ill-defined future. We can develop the wisdom to see how our childish, craving, envy-driven, hedonistic subminds lead us toward insatiable desires that leave us unhappy with our present life. And we can use techniques like meditation and contemplation to learn when we are controlling our minds, and when our subminds are controlling us.

If you are still skeptical about your ability to change your mind and the way you think, and to control your primitive, childish, petulant, self-absorbed, insatiable sub-minds, it may be useful to briefly mention the now recognized phenomenon of what is called *neuroplasticity*—the ability of the brain to change. In the past, scientists believed the adult brain was fully established and could not anatomically, physiologically, or functionally change. It is now recognized that this was incorrect, and that the brain can change in terms of growing new neuronal connections and "re-wiring" itself. The neurons in the brain can and do develop new connections to other neurons. The more certain thoughts or ways of thinking are practiced (e.g., optimism, positive outlook, mindfulness), the stronger these new connections become. You can actually change the way you think.

Electroencephalography (EEG) has shown that with meditation you can actually change the brain waves in your head. Changes in how the brain thinks and what parts of the brain think have been shown over and over again using a technique called functional MRI, which images in real time what parts of a person's brain is thinking at any moment. Brain MRI's also show that long-term meditation seems to lead not only to changes in the brain regions associated with emotions, such as anxiety, depression, fear and anger, but to the actual growth of gray matter and enlargement of certain areas of the brain (known as *neurogenesis*). The bottom line is that we can learn to control and train our brain and our mind to think differently, and for the better.

CHAPTER 4

THOUGHTS
AND EMOTIONS

According to *thebreathproject.org*, the average person has an astonishing 60,000 thoughts a day, and ninety percent of them are the same repetitive musings playing over and over. While thoughts—and the thinking that produces a thought—are obviously necessary to function in this world, it is also thoughts, generated by our many subminds. that hijack control of our mind. They inhibit our ability to be in and stay in the present moment, and thwart us from being in our natural-born state of happiness and inner peace.

To better control our thoughts, our first step is to recognize that we do not, for the vast majority of time we are awake, consciously generate our own thoughts. Rather, our subminds are always at work, trying to capture our mind's attention, obsessed with their own wants, fears, anxieties, aversions, and desires that generate thoughts.

As evolutionary psychologist Robert Wright (as well as many others) has observed:

> *Thoughts think themselves.*
> *Thoughts are directed*
> *towards the conscious,*
> *not from the conscious.*

Wright's words might sound heretical to you, but this is a simple truth. Rather than simply reading and trying to intellectualize this concept, it is best you realize this experientially. As I suggested to you before, sit for a few minutes and try to think of nothing, nothing at all. You may be able to make it twenty, thirty, or sixty seconds, but you will not be able to make it even a few minutes before some random thought pops into your conscious mind. Perhaps it will be a frustration from the morning, perhaps it will be thinking of an upcoming chore, job or trip. Perhaps it will be something seemingly completely random from last week, last month, or years past. Try this several times. The thoughts may be different, but the result will always be the same.

It is our subminds, or if you prefer to call it our sub-conscious, that generates the vast majority of our daily thoughts. Perhaps our ego submind is still upset about some perceived slight from months ago and just can't let it go. Or our worry submind can't stop agonizing over an upcoming meeting, or our hedonistic submind can't wait to scarf down yet another bowl of ice cream.

If you're still not convinced, ponder the last time an unpleasant or frustrating event occurred. It could be a fight you had with your partner or child, a snub from your neighbor, a financial setback, or something your parents chastised you about. Although you no doubt tried to forget the incident, your mind kept obsessing over it. Surely, you would not consciously choose to mull over and over this frustrating event, but it happens nonetheless. If you truly controlled your thoughts, however, you would choose not to think about it and move on, but for most of us, this is not something we are able to do consistently. Why? Because for the most part, throughout our daily lives, we cannot and do not control most of our thoughts.

The same goes for emotions. With our untrained minds, we are incapable of instantaneously stopping ourselves from becoming frustrated, sad, anxious, upset, or angry—though wouldn't it be great if we could?

The second step to taking back control of our mind is to recognize the thoughts we're having in real time. This is a key part, and benefit of, mindfulness—being in the present moment and becoming aware of what we're thinking and feeling. For example, in moments of exasperation, we can recognize that our frustration is growing. As we become irritated, we can recognize our anger is building. The same goes with something like binge eating in response to anger. We can recognize how this emotional desire is building and trying to take over our mind—and thereby resist woofing down an 800-calorie slab of cake.

We control our thoughts by recognizing them as they occur and recognizing that they are just a thought, nothing more. We do not have to accede to every thought we have. Just because a thought suggests we do something, doesn't mean we must obey it. Psychologist Lynn Rossy, in her wonderful book on mindful eating, writes:

> *Thoughts have no power,*
> *except the power you give them.*

A clever way to recognize an emotion as just an emotion is to view the emotion as separate from us. Joseph Goldstein, a leading expert and writer on mindfulness, suggests we identify the emotion as an emotion and something that is simply occurring in the present moment. Instead of saying to yourself that you are frustrated, take the approach of objectively and dispassionately thinking, or inwardly saying to yourself, that *frustration is present* or *frustration is occurring*. Instead of thinking that you are angry, recognize that *anger is present*. This approach of emotion X is present gives us the power to recognize the emotion, to dissociate the emotion from ourselves and keep it at arm's length, and then to thoughtfully and calmly deal with it. This method isolates or quarantines the emotion, and thus prevents the emotion from taking control of our mind. In the illustration on the following page, a woman depersonalizes her sense of growing frustration and instead thinks to herself *there is frustration,* preventing it from taking over her mind.

When you begin to experience a strong emotion such as anger, you can then ask yourself, Why am I experiencing this emotion? In some cases, we will realize that our emotional response is out of proportion to whatever little thing has occurred. We can then ask ourselves, Is it really that monumental of an event? We can also put the incident in perspective, Will I even remember this in a year from now? Or, is it so important that I should ruin my entire day over it?

It is also helpful to be able to recognize when your mind has been already taken over by a negative thought or emotion, be it sadness, frustration, worry, envy, annoyance, or anger. Lynn Rossy suggests we strive to recognize when we are in what she calls "bad thought mode." Simply being able to recognize when our mind has shifted into bad thought mode can allow us to pause, take a few breaths,

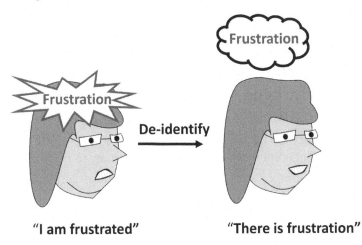

"I am frustrated"   "There is frustration"

and consider what triggered this state; assess how we are currently acting in response to the thought; and contemplate what we might be able to do to get out of bad thought mode. This is particularly helpful if, for example, we've begun to argue with someone. Any negative expressions will no doubt antagonize, or further antagonize, the person we are speaking with, adding fuel to the fire. As Will Rogers famously said,

If you find yourself in a hole,
the first thing to do is stop digging.

The same thing goes when our mind has been manipulated by some random person, event, or recollection into bad thought mode. The first thing to do is to recognize this and strive to not work ourselves up, or our partners/parents/children/boss, into even more of a lather.

Central to many of our undesirable emotions is the desire to blame someone. There is an often told teaching that if you are in a boat on a lake and another boat, driven by someone, drifts into and even grazes your boat, your mind is immediately filled with negative thoughts and emotions of indignation and anger toward that person. These negative emotions take over your mind. Now, picture the same scenario, only this time the boat that grazed your boat has no one in it—perhaps it became unmoored from a dock. In this case, you may likely react with momentary mild surprise but nothing more. We have to keep reminding ourselves that sometimes things just happen, or to paraphrase Forrest Gump: "*In life, shit happens.*" There isn't always someone to blame, and most of the time, even if there is a someone, they were most likely not consciously plotting to cause you harm or distress.

Another helpful strategy suggested by experts is to recognize that a thought is just a thought, not a fact. It is nothing more. Thoughts have no mass, no body, no form, and no substance. They are like transient clumps of foam or bubbles on the ocean's surface, ephemerally forming and disappearing into the ether. How then can you get mad at a thought? This is particularly helpful when one is thinking about something that *might* happen in the future, and your anger or indignation submind starts to rev into overdrive. Do you really want to ruin your mood and your day because of some abstract thought about something that may or may not happen in the future?

Pema Chödrön, an ordained American Buddhist nun and author who has triumphed over much adversity, counsels that whenever you find yourself caught in an emotional attack, ask yourself:

> *How much of this is really happening*
> *on the outside,*
> *and how much of this is in my mind?*

There is perhaps no harder thing for us to do in our daily lives than to stop perseverating on some recent event, frustration, argument, or slight. Many years ago, early in my career, I ran a committee tasked with improving the health of patients. We had many meetings and conference calls, and at the end of some I found myself quite frustrated. Though all involved were well-intentioned, my human frailty nonetheless led to exasperation with those I perceived as hindering, or even obstructing, my plans and agenda which, in my mind at least, were clearly (!) the best way forward. Try as I might, I simply could not shake these negative thoughts. I would repeatedly ponder why were they doing this? Could they not see that my vision was correct? What discussions, unbeknownst to me, were taking place to thwart my plans?

This was clearly not equanimous, or probably even rational thinking, but it occurred nonetheless. My exasperation, frustration, and ego subminds were out in force and try as I might, I simply could not subdue them. My evening walk with my dogs, instead of a pleasurable experience, was subverted by these recurring thoughts and emotions. During dinner with Lydia, when I should have been enjoying quality time with her, my mind was instead similarly subverted by these overpowering thoughts. Even my attempts at peaceful sleep were thwarted by these negative thoughts. What a moron I was. What a waste of my time, my day, and my night. If only I had been able to recognize these thoughts as only thoughts, not actual facts, and move beyond them. If only I had taken these thoughts, which burned in my mind like a hot ember, and snuffed them out.

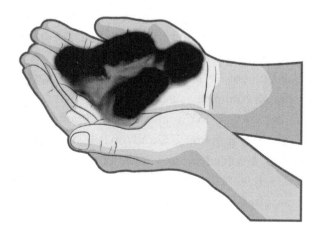

Would you continue to hold a red-hot coal in your hand? Of course not! But this is exactly what we do when we continue to replay a bad memory, thought, or interaction in our head. The more we do this, the more it burns us. Instead of putting it down, or letting the thought or emotion go, we continue to carry it with us. So the next time you find yourself in a similar situation, remind yourself to drop these thoughts, like red-hot coals.

As Pema Chödrön has observed:

> *We have a choice in any moment to either return to the present or to escalate our suffering by letting our stories and thoughts take over.*

This is a powerful message. Repeatedly ruminating on negative thoughts from the past (and *everything* that has already happened, even minutes ago, is now in the past) only leads to more suffering. The antidote for breaking this vicious cycle is to recognize what has taken over your mind and to refocus your thoughts on the present—what is happening right here and now. To do this, you must *really* focus though. Focus on your breath, on your footsteps, on the wind, the color of the sky, and the sounds around you. Focus on your good health (or at least being alive). Focus on the fact that right now you have a place to live; a job; a family; good friends; loving pets. There truly is so much good—right here, right now—in the present moment.

So why don't you

> *Take a break from the past,*
> *and a vacation from the future,*
> *and just be in the present.*

Put more succinctly, why don't you adopt the strategy to

> *Come back to the now, and*
> *abide in the present.*

Many of our negative thoughts and emotions have to do with unpleasant past interactions—disagreements and quarrels—with family members, friends, coworkers, and even strangers. We replay over and over how we would change what we said, sometimes wishing we'd been kinder or more skillful, or how we would show them who is smarter, wiser, or even righteous. We need to stop mulling over the past. There are no reruns in life. There are no redoes in life. That discussion we had years, months, days, hours, or even minutes ago is gone and done, and will never happen again no matter how many times we replay it in our heads. It has been washed down the river of life by the ever-flowing current of time, is no longer in our present, and will never be in our future. Wave goodbye as it vanishes from your consciousness. Better yet, metaphorically flush it down the toilet.

In Isaiah 43:18, we are advised to

> *Forget the former things;*
> *do not dwell on the past.*

Or, as Dr. Spencer Johnson, author of the best-selling book *Who Moved My Cheese*, observes:

Life moves on and so should we.

I listened to a podcast interview with Guy Armstrong, an insightful meditation expert and teacher, who noted that for some things, such as unpleasant or frustrating past memories:

We think think think
think think think about it.

The line basically sums up how we continue to flog ourselves over past interactions with others. It might be helpful to ask yourself, What do I think think think think think think about?

There is a famous Zen story about two monks traveling together who reach the banks of a river. As they are about to cross, they encounter a young woman who is also about to cross, though it will ruin her clothes and shoes. The monks look at each other, as they have taken vows never to touch a woman. The elder monk nonetheless picks up the woman on his back and carries her across the river. The younger monk looks on with a disturbed countenance. An hour passes, and he says nothing to the elder monk. Two, then three hours pass, and still he utters not a word, though he is clearly upset. Finally, the younger monk says in an impetuous tone to the elder monk: "How could you do such a thing as carry that woman across the river?!" The elder monk calmly replies: "I long ago put that woman down. Why do you still insist on carrying her around?"

33

Why do we keep carrying around such frustrations, vexations, indignations, and heavy mental loads? We would not choose to load up a backpack with heavy rocks, then strap it to our back and spend the entire day needlessly carrying it around. So why not figuratively take off that heavy backpack. Visualize yourself casting it off, only imagine the backpack loaded with weighty negative thoughts and emotions of an incident long past and no longer in the present.

While there are no reruns or replays in life, what we can do, to borrow a sports phrase, is do a *make-up call*. Reach out to the person with whom you've had an argument. Discuss your regrets (assuming you have some) and apologize, if necessary. A wise aphorism to keep in mind:

> *Apologizing doesn't always mean that you're wrong and the other person is right. It just means that you value your relationship more than your ego.*

So go ahead and apologize. You will feel like a weight has been lifted. You will bring closure to this regret and free yourself from the load you are carrying.

In order to take back control of our minds, we must understand how our minds can become hijacked by random thoughts; how our minds can become so adversely affected by something (e.g., a thought) that isn't real or even an actual fact, but is just a thought; and how even the slightest event, occurrence, or single spoken sentence can set our subminds ablaze with emotions that commandeer our inner peace. We need to learn to leave the past in the past, live in the present, and not worry about an unpredictable and unknown future. We must drop the hot coals of negative thoughts, which only feed upon themselves, and cast off emotions and feelings that do not serve us well.

CHAPTER 5

MINDFULNESS

T he term *mindfulness* is perhaps one of the least understood and over-commercialized words in the spiritual, self-help universe. Many of us are interested in being a little more *mindful*—even if we don't know what it really means. Yet, mindfulness is the single most important factor in taking back control of your mind and your life.

Although you'll find an infinite number of definitions of mindfulness—just do a quick google search—at its core mindfulness is *the present awareness of our thoughts, actions, and emotions.* It is the moment-to-moment awareness of where we are, what we are doing, and what we are thinking.

Mindfulness is the ability to recognize in real time an emotion you are experiencing, such as when you are beginning to feel frustrated. It is the ability to recognize and identify who or what is making you frustrated; and to then be able to pause *before* you start to allow your mind or your frustration submind to *react*. And, it is the ability to skillfully see the path, or course of action, you can take to avoid compounding or escalating your frustration, or even better to avoid frustration entirely.

We have already discussed how most people—you included—believe, or contend, that they are (of course!) always aware of what they are thinking; what they are feeling; what they are consciously deciding to say or do. But this is not so, and most of us are not aware. Our minds are on autopilot, passively being moved, minute-by-minute, by what neurophysiologists call our brain's *default mode network,* which in modern lingo is the brain's background operating system.

A good example of this concept is when you are on a long drive across state or even going to work. You may be listening to music, the radio, or daydreaming about dinner or an upcoming vacation. Your eyes may be pointed ahead towards the road, but your mind is elsewhere – on work, on dinner, on a distant memory or upcoming trip. Yet, you somehow turn the steering wheel just enough as the road bends to the left and stay in your lane for hours at a time. Think about all those slight corrections your hands make to stay in the middle of the lane. You are not constantly telling yourself, "OK, turn two degrees to the left, now back one degree to the right, now keep the steering wheel perfectly still." Some background program deep in your brain is instinctively making all these constant small adjustments. You are not consciously doing them—it is your mind's default mode network doing this. It is only if you see an accident up ahead or an animal in the road that you are jarred into a state of mindfulness and take conscious control of the steering wheel to navigate the upcoming obstacle. Only for these few seconds are you really mindfully driving.

How many times a day are you actually *aware* of what your mind is thinking, feeling, or reacting to? This is different than just *experiencing* a thought, emotion, or interaction with another person. Taken further, how many times can you remember actually being aware of being aware? To better understand this concept of mindfulness and of being aware, take the twenty-four hour awareness challenge. See how many times over the next day you are able to pause and recognize a moment when you are truly aware of what you are thinking and what is going on around you. Aware—in real time—of who and how you are interacting with another person. How many times can you recognize that you are aware of being aware at that very moment? I would wager it will be fewer than the number of fingers on one hand. This is the amount of time during a twenty-four hour period you are actually being mindful. The results, I am pretty sure, will both surprise and disappoint you.

In *The Mind Illuminated*, Dr. John Yates discusses the concept of *introspective awareness*. In simple terms, introspective awareness is the ability to be aware of and to observe our thoughts, feelings, and emotions. While we all no doubt would respond that we know, for instance, when we are angry, the problem is that we only note this after the fact, when we've escalated an argument or worked ourselves up. It is infinitely more useful to be able to sense when we are about to become upset or frustrated, or when we are making ourselves sad by repeatedly replaying in our minds an upsetting memory. This is a key benefit of introspective awareness. It is also useful to more generally identify how one is feeling, as this will help us, as we will discuss in later chapters, to deal with negative emotions.

Metacognitive Introspective Awareness

John Yates also explains the concept of what he calls *metacognitive introspective awareness*—the ability to observe not only one's thoughts and feelings but the activity and overall state of one's mind. It is as if you are able to step outside your skull and watch your brain think.

Introspective awareness and metacognitive introspective awareness may seem like abstract words on paper. But these two abilities exist and are something you can become better at, as they are key aspects of mindfulness. To paraphrase from the website mindful.org, mindfulness is "waking up to the inner workings of our mind," which is what these types of awarenesses are all about. Meditation is the best way to truly understand these concepts, to comprehend them experientially, and to begin to grow your skills in being aware of your thoughts, emotions, and what your mind is thinking. If you're not ready to try formal meditation, then just sit for a few minutes and explore the state of your mind's emotions, or see if you can just observe your thoughts as your mind jumps from one random thought to another. Do this, and consider just how cool it will be to tell your partner, friends, and family members that you have metacognitive introspective awareness!

Mindfulness is a powerful skill and ally in our quest to take back control of our minds. Rather than, when we are having a conversation, reflexively and mindlessly blurting out some unskillful speech or the first words that occur to us (e.g., "You're an idiot!"), mindfulness allows us to listen deeply to what someone is saying, and then contemplate how we should respond to them *before* we reply. This allows us to be aware of what we say and to tactfully phrase a response. Mindfulness allows us to monitor our thoughts and our mischievous subminds, especially if a submind is trying to get us to think or do something detrimental to our mental and physical well-being or hurtful to someone else. Mindfulness allows us to sense negative emotions or reactions that build up inside our mind and alerts us to take mental steps to mitigate such feelings or memories. In short, mindfulness acts as a circuit breaker between our many misbehaving, impish, naughty, self-centered, and misguided subminds and our conscious thoughts, feelings, emotions, actions, and reactions.

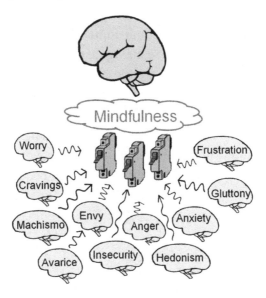

Unfortunately, you cannot just buy mindfulness (though a search on Amazon for *mindfulness* yielded over 80,000 items for sale!). You can't get it from a book, a magazine article, a lecture, or by passively listening to a course or podcast on the subject. While reading and hearing about mindfulness is helpful to better understand it, you ultimately need to develop it yourself, experientially. And this comes, at least initially, from meditation practice or dedicated time off-the-grid to practice mindfulness exercises. Initial mindfulness practices or exercises include awareness of the breath, open and non-judgmental monitoring of your mind's thoughts, systematic "body scans" of your entire body, or doing a walking meditation (focusing on each step). We will discuss some simple mindfulness exercises later in the book. Once you better understand how to watch and monitor your thoughts during meditation or a comparable practice, you can then gradually expand this process from just twenty minutes on the meditation cushion to 24/7 in the real world.

In order to take back control of our mind, we must understand how it reacts and thinks. Mindfulness allows us to chart our own course, navigate the road bumps in the highways of life, and to decide how we want to respond (not react) to these infinite occurrences, interactions, and situations that are part of everyday life. So, if you truly want to be more mindful, don't just buy the latest magazine that has mindfulness plastered across its cover, but rather commit to actively invest time to practice becoming more mindful.

CHAPTER 6

RAIN AND RAID

Once you begin to understand and develop mindfulness, you can use it to great advantage to help control your mind's reactions to the infinite events and frustrations of everyday life. A mindfulness strategy that has become popular over the last two decades is **RAIN** (an acronym reportedly first coined by the expert meditation and mindfulness teacher Michele McDonald). The **RAIN** strategy has four steps:

1. Recognize
2. Accept
3. Investigate
4. Non-identify

Let's break these down one by one.

Recognize is the most practical and important step. What this means is that when a situation plays out in real time, like your kid trying to push your buttons by not eating her dinner or a work colleague seeming to disrespect you, you are able to recognize within yourself feelings of annoyance, frustration, exasperation, or anger starting to build up. You may literally say to yourself something along the lines of, "This is starting to piss me off" or "There he goes again!" This ability to recognize what is happening in the moment allows you to take a deep breath, regroup, and try to stop the emotional train before it builds up more and more steam, careens out of control, and goes off the rails.

Once you recognize that some person, occurrence, or situation is starting to lead to an unwanted negative emotional response, your next step is to *Accept* that this is happening. Others define the **A** as standing for *Allow*, as in just *Allow* the emotion to be there. We know we can't fight a building emotion and repress it with blunt force—no matter how many times we may tell ourselves not to let something bother us. We don't have to like what is happening, but we can at least accept what is happening. So rather than fight the emotion or feeling, we accept it.

Once we accept that something is starting to rub us the wrong way, we can now get down to the business of truly understanding what is happening in our mind by *Investigating* the situation. What is it that has set us off? Why are we reacting—or overreacting—to what someone said or did? Was it really so malicious? Is there something in our personality, or past experiences, that is causing us to react the way we are? Are we just tired or anxious? Did they really mean to piss us off with what they said or did? Or perhaps this is just a misunderstanding or some unintentional consequence of them not having spoken or acted skillfully?

Non-identification is perhaps the hardest step to understand. It seems to derive from Buddhist concepts of what the self is, or rather, what the self is not—an abstract concept I have spent years trying to better comprehend. I, therefore, prefer to change the acronym to **RAID**, with the **D** standing for *Depersonalize*. I use this in two senses. First, as we have discussed, we tend to have extremely egocentric views of the world, seeing everything that is happening across seven continents, vast oceans, billions of people, and trillions of stars and galaxies, all in terms of I, me, mine. How does this affect *me*? We think to ourselves that some person's glance, word, or action must have been directed at *me*, with the explicit purpose of pissing *me* off. For example, we might think to ourselves, That jerk who swerved into my lane was intentionally trying to cut in front of *me*!

It is helpful to recognize that sometimes things just happen, or people say or take actions not directly aimed at you. They have their own feelings, worries, and desires, and may say or do things to address their issues, and may not be skillful enough to perceive or predict how their actions affect you as "collateral damage." To depersonalize, in this sense, is helpful in pacifying or at least de-escalating any reaction your ego or machismo subminds may have to a particular occurrence or circumstance.

A second approach is to depersonalize the feeling, emotion, or reaction itself. You, or your "self," is not just any and every emotion that happens to instantaneously occur as a reaction to external events. You are not the frustration that may occur if the waiter brings you the wrong entree, or the anger that pops into your head if you are stood up on a date. These are not you; they are simply emotions. As we discussed earlier, mindfulness and stress experts suggest that rather than thinking *I am frustrated* or *I am angry*, acknowledge the emotion first; in this case, frustration or anger. With this approach, you view the emotion as something that is occurring external to yourself, which keeps the emotion at arm's length. You do not identify with it, but rather depersonalize it. With this approach, it is much easier to not become entangled with the emotion, like a fly stuck in a spider's web, but rather to accept the emotion and recognize that, in time, be it minutes or hours, it will inevitably pass.

RAIN or **RAID** helps us from becoming knocked off-kilter by the inevitable events and personal interactions that are part of life. It helps us, when these situations arise, to take back control of our minds from the primitive submind reactions of frustration, anger, and worry. So the next time you are faced with one of life's endless challenges, think about these steps:

1. **R**ecognize
2. **A**ccept
3. **I**nvestigate
4. **D**epersonalize

CHAPTER 7

CRAVINGS

I n Buddhist philosophy, it is recognized that unhappiness, discontent, and suffering derive directly from what are generically called and categorized as *cravings*. The craving to have something one does not possess. The craving for some particular person to like you and date you (or marry you). The craving to be, or live, in someplace other than where you are right now (e.g., a bigger home, a tropical island). The craving for a different job or career. The craving to be skinnier or prettier (or more muscular or handsome). The craving to have a flashier car, fancier clothes, a bigger diamond ring, or the latest and greatest iPhone.

Where there is craving, there is unhappiness and discontentment. Where there is no craving, there is happiness and inner peace.

A reasonable synonym for craving is desire. And our desires are insatiable. If we get one bite of cake, we want a second, then a third. A year after we get an iPhone 7, we want an iPhone 8 (or iPhone X or iPhone 11). After we get a sixty-inch flat screen TV, we then want a seventy-five-inch flat screen TV. If we have a three bedroom house, we want a five bedroom house. As soon as we get promoted to assistant manager, we want to be associate manager.

In *The Path of Insight Meditation*, authors Joseph Goldstein and Jack Kornfield have written the following about trying to satisfy our endless cravings:

> *It is like trying to quench your thirst*
> *by drinking ocean water.*
> *The more you drink, the thirstier you*
> *become.*

The more you get into the habit of constantly acceding to and feeding your cravings, the more they arise, and the more power and control they exert over you and your mind. The more your craving subminds learn that they will always get what they want if they just keep crying out for more and more, loud and long enough, the greater their proclivity to continue to cry out. As Sakyong Mipham has craftily noted:

> *Desire is a creature*
> *with an endless appetite.*

And your craving subminds are *very* hungry!

The Buddhists describe a horrific realm in the wheel of life called that of the *hungry ghosts*. These poor beings have insatiable hunger yet have pin-wide long necks and are thus never able to eat enough to satisfy their unquenchable appetite. They are doomed to endless suffering and unhappiness.

48

You probably get the analogy. They represent how we behave—as if we are one of these poor hungry ghosts. Why not, instead of endlessly craving more and more, take stock of and appreciate what we already have. Why not

> *Think about what you have,*
> *instead of what you want.*

What happens when we don't get what we are craving? We pout and become petulant, irritable, or morose, wallowing in our own misery. We feel sorry for ourselves. We decry the world is not fair. Our craving subminds have, over the years, become accustomed to getting their own way and vindictively create havoc and suffering in our minds when they don't get all that they want.

Author Timber Hawkeye, who gave up life in the fast lane and now leads a simple, happier life, sums up this concept beautifully:

> *Your mind is like a spoiled rich kid!*
> *You have raised it to think whatever*
> *it wants, whenever it wants to, and*
> *for however long, with no regard for*
> *consequences or gratitude.*

TAKE BACK CONTROL OF YOUR MIND

Now that your mind is all grown, it
never listens to you.

Please reflect a moment on that first line: "Your mind is like a spoiled rich kid." Most of us have enough, and some (particularly those in poor, third world countries or even those who live in poverty in the U.S.) would opine we have more than enough. Yet, we all want more, more, more. And when we don't get it, there is disappointment, discontentment, and suffering.

There is a great cartoon I came across of the Dalai Lama receiving a birthday gift box from some Buddhist monks. The Dalai Lama opens the box and sees that it is empty. He proclaims, with great delight: "Just what I always wanted . . . nothing!" You cannot be disappointed with not getting what you never craved. You cannot fall into the envy trap for that which you do not desire. If you do not get what you do not want, you will never be sad.

While we do not want to get too philosophical, it is worthwhile to mention the Tibetan monk Mingyur Rinpoche's take on cravings. To paraphrase him:

> *Cravings are the misguided belief that*
> *there is something wrong with the*
> *present moment.*

The implication is that we have everything we need right now to be happy, yet we want something to be different than it is. Can we really not be happy right now and with what we have unless we have that fancier watch, bigger TV, seven-layer cake, latest designer jeans, job promotion, boyfriend, lifestyle, fame, or ocean-front mansion?

Don't get me wrong about cravings. We are all glad to have the things necessary for a good life (a home, transportation, adequate clothes, and food) and some nice material possessions. It is unrealistic to expect us to give up all our desires and live like monks in a cave. And it is not a sign of gluttony or depravity if we are happy when we do get a new smartphone, piece of jewelry, new dress or suit, or TV. Heck, I'll admit that I have sixteen pairs of cowboy boots (that's a lot even for someone who lives in Texas!). The key difference is between being glad to get something and craving something. An attitude of "It will be nice if years down the road we can afford a bigger house, so let's spend less now to save up for it" is quite different from "I want a bigger house now, and I will not be happy until we get it." It may thus be helpful, when the occasion arises, to ask oneself:

What do I need, and what do I crave?

- A place to live? Sounds like that makes the "need" category.
- Adequate income to feed the family and pay the bills? Yep, the need category.
- Warm clothes? The need category.
- New state-of-the-art deep base surround sound stereo system? It would be nice, but this falls into the "cravings" category. If I get it—great. If not, no worries.

When a craving arises, the mindful approach is to first *recognize* the urge as a craving and to label it as such. The simple act of recognizing that an urge or desire is a craving and not some life-essential staple is more than half the battle. In mindfulness practice, we do not try to suppress or ignore these feelings, as it is impossible for you—and your mind—to do so. Rather, we recognize a craving as just that—a craving—like any other thought. It is not a fact; it is not an object with mass, color, or texture; it is just a massless thought. Examine your desire or fixation: Why do I really want this? Where did this craving come from? Will I really be happier if I get it? Will I have total happiness when I get it? (I hope, by now, you recognize that the answer is an emphatic "no.")

We can also recognize that some cravings, like other thoughts or feelings, are transient and will likely pass within the next few minutes, hours, or at worst days. I try, with varying degrees of success, to use this approach when I get my late night craving for a few bites of anything unhealthy to eat (the ultimate "wasted extra calories," as my wife reminds me). It doesn't work all the time, but at least it works some of the time. When it does work, or when I am disciplined enough to give it a chance, I'll notice that within a minute or two, the craving passes. I can then settle back down for the night minus the several hundred extra calories I would have stuffed into my mouth.

These small victories are helpful in the larger scheme of things in that it is training my many craving subminds that it is I—not them—who is in control of what I think and do. My mind is learning that my many uncontrollable urges are actually controllable. We need to win small battles before we can win big wars. So a great first step is to see if you can overcome smaller cravings. For example, what "softball" (easy to overcome) cravings can you mindfully recognize, deal with, diffuse, and resist?

Our craving submind is powerful and insatiable, like a hungry ghost. It is always on the lookout for new things to crave and is never satisfied. It shouts at us, pleads with us, cries out to us, and tries to cajole us. It tries to take control of our mind, our thoughts, and our very being. But we can overcome our craving submind. We can recognize that it is crying out with yet another craving. We can learn to recognize the difference between what we need and what we crave. We can recognize that as much as this spoiled-little-child-craving submind moans and groans, the thought or desire it produces will likely pass. We can watch in our minds this craving impulse begin and grow and recognize that if we do not embrace it, it will ultimately pass. We can take back from our craving subminds control of our mind.

CHAPTER 8

HAPPINESS
AND UNHAPPINESS

The word and concept of *happiness* is omnipresent throughout modern society in what we hear and read, and our culture is obsessed with finding it. Songs such as "Happy," "Don't Worry, Be Happy," "Happy Together," and "If You Wanna Be Happy." Books such as *The Art of Happiness*, *Authentic Happiness*, and *The Happiness Project*. A TV show called *Happy Days*. Even our U.S. Declaration of Independence declares that we have an inalienable right to the pursuit of happiness. We all want to be happy, and we spend the majority of our lives in pursuit of this goal.

But what actually is happiness? Does simply being in a positive mental state such as contentment qualify, or does one need to be experiencing intense joy or pleasure? Does simply feeling good constitute happiness? If so, is a person who snorts cocaine and gets high every day happy? Is being happy necessarily having wealth, a spouse, or children? Is happiness simply the absence of negative thoughts and emotions?

Dan Harris, an ABC newscaster and meditation convert, wrote an entertaining and educational book he titled *10% Happier*. It's a great read, but raises the question: ten percent happier than what? How does one quantify happiness if we cannot even define or identify what it is? Our three dogs—though a handful—give me great happiness, but I'm not so sure adopting a fourth dog will make me thirty-three percent happier!

Interestingly, when I google *happiness*, I get a potpourri of definitions and criteria, including "a state of well-being and contentment"; "the state of feeling or showing pleasure"; "a state of joy"; "the quality of being happy"; and "the feeling of being pleased." None of these really seem to illuminate what happiness really is.

But when I google *true happiness*, its predominant definition is along the lines of "a mind at peace." Now this seems something to strive for! I can tell you that at times during my meditative practice, when I am choosing to focus the meditation very narrowly on thinking of nothing but the breath, or better yet thinking nothing at all, there is an incredible feeling that arises of what I would characterize as inner peace. No worries, no concerns, no desires, no frustrations, no anxieties, no regrets, no thoughts, nothing. Nothing that is, except this extraordinary peaceful feeling. Now this is not being a mindless, surgically decorticated zombie, like what they did to Jack Nicholson's character in *One Flew over the Cuckoo's Nest*, but simply a feeling free of all negative thoughts, worry, self-doubt, and cravings. That, perhaps, is what is meant by "a mind at peace" and is an example of true happiness.

Many people think of happiness as if it were something attainable in the future, if only they had a better car, bigger house, sexier girlfriend, higher paying job, or more caring boyfriend. It is not something achievable now, but will be once one is finally able to obtain the material possessions one craves or finds the perfect partner or reaches retirement. This does not seem the most skillful approach to life and is contrary to the belief that once one better understands and controls the mind, one can be happy right here, right now.

Along these lines, it is interesting to examine the difference between what people crave or desire in the abstract future to make them happy, and what people actually answer when asked to list what brings them happiness now.

In rough order, according to one poll, the things people list that do bring them happiness are (1) family and relationships; (2) meaningful work; and (3) positive thinking (e.g., satisfaction with life, gratefulness). Other things high on the list include giving to others, religion, personal freedom, and good health. Interestingly, things that some people think will bring them happiness, such as fame, fortune, and beauty, are nowhere to be found on that list of what actually makes people happy. Neither is a newer smartphone, a shinier car, a bigger house, a sexier girlfriend, or many of the other things we tend to crave.

There's such a thing—really—as the *World Happiness Report*. The factors used in this report to assess well-being include healthy life expectancy; social support; freedom; trust; generosity; and income. Of these six criteria, only one has anything to do with money. What are the happiest countries in the world? According to this report, Finland, Denmark, Norway, Iceland, and the Netherlands are the top five—not exactly countries known for wealth or opulence. The materialistic and wealthy United States comes in a pathetic nineteenth, below countries such as Costa Rica and

Luxembourg. Yikes! Seems all our American wealth, technology, and opulence doesn't buy or guarantee happiness.

Perhaps it is useful to make a list of the things you *think* you need to have in order to be happy. After you are done, then make another list of the things currently in your life that you already have that actually do bring you happiness. It would be informative to compare the two lists.

There are an infinite number of definitions of unhappiness, but the one I think most useful is "a state characterized by emotions ranging from mild discontent to deep grief" (as defined on, of all places, crosswordsolver.com). Let's focus on the "discontent" part, since this is a subjective attitude and thus, in theory, controllable and changeable. Discontent has, in turn, been defined as a "lack of satisfaction with one's possessions, status, or situation." Again, note that it is not the number of possessions, social or work status, or personal or professional situation per se, but rather one's subjective choice not to be satisfied with what one currently has.

Chris Prentiss, author of *Zen and the Art of Happiness*, wrote the following:

> *It is the way you look at things,*
> *and the way you relate to them,*
> *that determines your state of*
> *happiness or unhappiness,*
> *not the things themselves.*

David Michie, the international best-selling author, similarly counsels:

58

HAPPINESS AND UNHAPPINESS

What we think about our
circumstances
is way more important
than the circumstances themselves.

What both of these authors are saying is that in any situation, with any amount of material possessions, with any job and any relationship, we have the choice to decide in our minds whether to see the glass as half full or half empty. Put another way, the glass may not be completely full, but it is full enough to be happy with what we have, and where we are in our lives.

The same holds for things that happen in our lives. As Prentiss writes,

> *An event is only an event.*
> *It's how we treat the event that*
> *determines what it becomes in our lives.*
> *The event doesn't make that*
> *determination—we do.*

I love that last line. The event doesn't decide if we are happy or unhappy as it is occurring, we—in our minds—decide. In the neighborhood where my wife and I live, there are a lot of little kids, and we would get invited to many of their birthday parties. Being in my 50s, and frankly loving dogs more than screaming kids, and despite the best intentions of our neighbors, I found these parties kind of boring. But note that it was my attitude and not the party itself that made what I perceived and experienced the parties to be, even when all the other neighbors were having a great time.

How we experience an event, how we perceive what we have, and how happy or unhappy we are, are determined by what we think, not what is. As the Dalai Lama so succinctly stated:

> *Once our basic survival needs are met,*
> *happiness is determined more by the*
> *state of our mind than by our external*
> *circumstances.*

Even more succinctly stated is what William Shakespeare wrote hundreds of years ago:

> *There is nothing either good or bad,*
> *but thinking makes it so.*

The point is, to at least a good extent, we control whether we are happy or unhappy. Yes, there are very real psychological conditions and events in life that cause depression and which often require counseling, therapy, and medications. But we are not talking about that here. Rather, we are talking about our everyday existence and our day-to-day lives.

As we discussed in the book's preface, Charles Swindoll, a twentieth-century Christian pastor, famously noted:

> *Life is 10% what happens to you,*
> *and 90% how you react to it.*

We can control some of the things that happen to us in life, but a lot of things we cannot. Things will happen. It's how we view them that determines our emotional state.

HAPPINESS AND UNHAPPINESS

Carlos Castaneda, one of the fathers of the New Age movement, who wrote of his training in Native American shamanism, wryly observed the following:

> *We can make ourselves miserable,*
> *or we can make ourselves happy.*
> *The amount of work is the same.*

So perhaps we should not obsessively seek out things to "make" ourselves happy. Perhaps we should take stock of what we have—our health, our friends, our family, a place to live, and enough food and water to survive—and just *be* happy.

Don't wait to be happy a year from now. Don't wait to be happy a week from now. Don't wait to be happy a day from now. Don't wait to be happy an hour from now. Be happy now.

As Thich Nhat Hanh has written:

> *Whether or not this moment is happy*
> *or not depends on you.*
> *It is you who makes the moment*
> *happy,*
> *not the moment that makes you*
> *happy.*

In fact, many believe that happiness is our natural state, and it is only our upbringing, society, and life itself that leads us to develop negative thought processes that keep knocking us off this pleasant perch. American physician and researcher Dean Ornish, in discussing his own spiritual journey in life on Oprah Winfrey's *Super Soul Sunday* series, noted that it was a turning point in his life when through meditation he realized that it is not what he needed to have or do in order to be happy, but what he needed to *stop* doing in order to stop disturbing the natural state of happiness that is already there.

You don't have to do something to be happy. You don't have to have something to be happy. You don't have to be somewhere to be happy. You can just allow yourself to *be* happy.

Perhaps our Western society has it all wrong. We keep looking for what we can *gain* to make us happy. Perhaps instead we focus on what we can *lose* to make us happy: our anxieties, our worries, and our cravings.

In summary, it may be hard to truly define happiness. But I do think that if we want to take greater control of our lives, it is still useful to sit down and devote serious time to contemplate what really makes us happy (or at least happier)—however we define it—and what we only think will, in some ill-defined future, magically make us happy. We can think about the things we have, rather than what we don't have. We can ponder the things that prevent us from being happy. We can begin to understand when our mind, and our happiness, is being subverted by our hedonism, gluttony, and envy subminds. We can use meditation or contemplation to improve how we think about things. As the Dalai Lama and psychiatrist Howard Cutler suggested in their book *The Art of Happiness*:

> *Working on our mental outlook is a more effective means of achieving happiness than seeking it through*

external sources such as wealth, position or even physical health.

CHAPTER 9

THE SECOND ARROW

In Buddhist teachings, there is a famous parable referred to as "the second arrow." As the story goes, you may one day be walking in a forest when suddenly you get hit by an arrow that grazes your skin (or in more modern terms, you may be walking down the city street and stub your toe on the sidewalk). The initial sensation of pain is your first, unavoidable reaction. This may last a few seconds. But then your second reaction may be frustration, annoyance, anger, or even rage. You then spend minutes—or hours—perseverating about who dared to shoot that arrow (or built that sidewalk uneven). You become obsessed with finding this person, what you will do when you confront this person, how you will scold this person, and what you will do to seek revenge and get even. The more you think, the more indignant, bilious, and embittered you become. It's like you are mentally throwing lighter fuel on the fire—feeding the flames of negativity, frustration, indignation, and anger. You have ruined your walk, your afternoon, and your day. You have shot yourself with the proverbial second arrow.

This metaphorical first arrow may not be what happened to us a few minutes ago, but may be something that happened this morning, yesterday, last week, or even months or years ago. How many perceived slights, insults, injuries, and injustices long past do we continue to carry around in our metaphorical quiver, shooting ourselves again and again with a second, third, or fourth arrow? How many times do we continue to work ourselves up, get frustrated, and grow angry about events long past, of which we cannot alter, no matter how many times we replay them in our mind. How many recent and past events do you carry around and repeat over and over in your mind? The person who cut you off while driving to work; the girlfriend who long ago broke up with you; the man at the fast food restaurant who seemed to cut in front of you; the boss who passed you up for a raise; the spouse who dismissed all the hard work you do to maintain the house?

These incidents and events that our machismo and ego subminds keep replaying in our minds, jabbing ourselves with arrows again and again, are long over. Allowing our subminds to keep jabbing these thoughts into our minds serves no purpose other than to compromise our equanimity. As Chris Prentiss writes:

> *Carrying that load of hurtful baggage*
> *from the past is a useless burden we*
> *would be much better off without.*

Why keep weighing yourself down with such thoughts? What purpose do they serve? Why not take the load off your back, put them down, and pull the arrow out of your soul.

I have found that a round of golf, at which I am mediocre but enjoy, provides more than ample opportunity for me to put this approach to life to the test. In golf, one devotes an entire Saturday or Sunday to playing a round. In theory, it should be an enjoyable day: spending time with good friends, sharing a cold beer or two, while enjoying the game in a beautiful setting. Yet, with every one of the seventy, eighty, ninety, or hundred or more (!) shots one takes, there is the potential to slice the ball into the woods, plunk it into the water, or blade (miss-hit) the shot clear over the green and into an unforgiving marsh. In fact, it is impossible not to play a round of golf without having this happen some (or even dozens) of times. Momentarily reacting with disappointment or frustration when this "first arrow" hits you is all but natural and inevitable. But it is in how you subsequently react that determines whether you enjoy the round of golf or squander an entire day engulfed and mired in frustration, disappointment, and anger.

Those who can accept these inevitable bad shots, shake them off, and move on, are rewarded with a relaxing, enjoyable, and glorious day. Those though who react to every one of these bad shots by becoming frustrated and enraged, shoot themselves again and again with second, third, and forth arrows. In fact, I've witnessed firsthand one of my friends, an extremely skilled golfer the likes of which I can only dream of, make *one* bad shot, then sit in his golf cart sulking the remainder of the round, while my buddy and I hack up the entire course and have a great time. My sulking friend not only shoots himself with a second arrow, he bashes himself over the head with an entire set of golf clubs.

Let's also remember that even these first arrows, if metaphorically left in the body and kept in our minds, will be a source of irritation and a nidus for disease to develop. When you get hit with an arrow, don't let it fester within, leading to infection, pus, and boils. Pluck it out and discard it, then forget about it and move on. My sulking golfer friend would have been well-served by such an approach!

In life, as the saying goes:

Pain is inevitable,
suffering is optional.

As we have already discussed, shit happens. It will happen to every one of us, and it will likely happen again and again. We cannot control the initial pain when these arrows of life hit us, but we can—when we take back control of our mind—control our reaction to it and take a pass on suffering.

Remember, our subminds will take these inevitable events of life as a cue and an invitation to act up, trying to make us feel frustration, anger, sadness, or indignation, and will seek to dictate and dominate our next thoughts and reactions. But we do not have to accede to them.

Mindfully, we can recognize and acknowledge our initial primitive and maladaptive thoughts, and understand that indulging them will only lead to more suffering. With this enlightened approach, we become able to move past our initial primitive instinctual reactions, and bring ourselves back into focusing on not what happened five minutes, five hours, or five days ago, but on what is happening now.

It may be useful to mentally practice your reaction to the first arrows you encounter daily by envisioning scenarios that set you off. Your partner leaving the bathroom messier than you consider clean, the inevitable traffic jam, the stubborn child, or the criticism from your unskillful boss or work colleague. Ask yourself, how did I react? How do I *want* to react? What will I try to do the next time this occurs? Devoting some time to this in the quiet of a meditative or contemplative session can be helpful.

So when we get hit with the inevitable first arrows of daily life, let's not shoot ourselves with a second arrow at every inevitable frustration, disappointment, and pain. Let's not overreact to things. Instead, let's try to acknowledge, accept, and not react at all. And let's certainly not bash ourselves over the head, adding additional suffering to our momentary pains. It takes skill and practice to recognize when our subminds are trying to assert themselves, but with practice and an understanding of our minds, we can avoid the second arrows of life and instead go on enjoying it.

69

CHAPTER 10

LIVE IN THE NOW

L iving in the now seems like such a simple and obvious concept, but we rarely do. Rather, we spend our lives thinking and living for the next weekend, our next vacation, or even retirement. Our mind is transfixed by the beguiling yet fallacious promise of imaginary future happiness, blinding us to enjoying what is happening now. Joseph Goldstein asks us to consider the following:

> *How often are we living in*
> *anticipation of what comes next,*
> *as if that will finally bring us to some*
> *sort of completion or fulfillment?*

What a simple yet profound insight. We spend most of our lives remembering the past and thinking about the future, but paying little or no heed to what is happening *now*. Similar sentiments are expressed by author and Buddhist teacher David Nichtern, in his book *Awakening from the Daydream*:

We spend much of our time stuck on
the treadmill of life, trying to get by,
to just make it through another day,
to make it to retirement. Then, before
we know it, the years go by, we get old
and sick, and then we die.

How often do you go through your daily ritual of wake, shower, dress, commute, work, go home, eat dinner, and sleep, without ever actually enjoying, savoring, or relishing even a minute of the day? How often, in your busy day, do you stop and enjoy the moment? How often do you turn off the constant barrage of thoughts from your subminds about perceived past injustices and of worries about the future? How often do you stop and smell the proverbial roses?

The mindlessly spent hours become mindlessly spent days. The mindlessly spent days become mindlessly spent years. The mindlessly spent years become mindlessly spent decades. The mindlessly spent decades become a mindlessly spent lifetime.
Then we die.

As meditation expert and teacher Guy Armstrong points out:

Past and future are only concepts.
They don't truly exist.
The past is gone, and the future
hasn't arrived.
What is real is the present moment.

Yet, we spend most of our time thinking, regretting, or worrying about the past or the future, instead of appreciating the present. What a waste of our limited time here on Earth. Speaking of wasted life, some people will waste a full five-sevenths of their life. How many of us live for the weekend? We grind away Monday through Friday, just hoping to make it to Saturday, when we can start to relax, have fun, and enjoy our lives. Monday is referred to as "moan day" and Wednesday as "hump day"—if we can just somehow manage to get over this hump, in a few more days the fun starts. If this is your attitude, with tunnel vision of only enjoying Saturdays and Sundays, then you are only living two-sevenths of your entire life. Doing the math, assuming you work from age eighteen to sixty-five, you are wasting 12,253 days of your life. That's 1,750 weeks and 408 months, or thirty-three years of your life! So don't just live two-sevenths of your life—live your entire life. Live every day.

Yes, we all have to work to make a living, or tend to the endless tasks of maintaining a home and raising children. But we do not want to write off five-sevenths of every week from our lives. We can still find at least some enjoyment from the tasks we do. And we can still treasure the fact that at least we are alive, because one day, perhaps a year from now, a week from now or tomorrow, we will no longer be. So, as we go about the many activities we do each day, think of it this way: *It's not stuff to do, it's stuff to experience.* Pretend this is the last day of your life.

Remember the caution Jim Morrison tells us in The Door's song "The Soft Parade":

> *All our lives we sweat and save,*
> *building for a shallow grave.*

73

We can prudently plan for the future. We can work for the future. But the time to live is now.

As Jim Rohn, the late entrepreneur and motivational speaker, said

> *Happiness is not something*
> *you postpone for the future.*

Where I work, one can "cash in" unused vacation days when one retires. At one point, I had about eighty unused days, and I would calculate in my head that big payout if I were to keep saving these unused vacation days until I retired. What a stupid strategy and approach to life! How do I know if I might get struck one day soon by some illness that would prevent me from enjoying my retirement years? How could I know for sure if I would even be alive by retirement age? Luckily, Lydia, who would observe how hard I worked, how much time I spent at the hospital, how much time I would spend traveling to meetings, and even how I would be attached to my computer doing catch-up work on weekends, implored me to bring a more balance to my life. Once a month, she suggested, I should take one of these so-called "precious" banked-up vacations days and create a three-day weekend for myself of uninterrupted quality time with loved ones, enjoy the house and the yard that we worked so hard to fix up; barbecue a few veggie burgers; unplug from my computer and just be. After all,

> *What is the point of being alive*
> *if you are not going to enjoy life?*

We all like to think of ourselves as free-thinking, independent beings, deciding for ourselves what we will do each day. But, to a great extent, that is not the case. Instead, we often act like mindless zombies sleepwalking through life. Hamsters on an ever-spinning hamster wheel. Gerbils mindlessly scurrying through endless plastic tubes in the Habitrail of life. We spin and spin, traveling through circumscribed pathways of life, going wherever the next Habitrail tube takes us, rarely pausing to enjoy the journey. What Lydia encouraged me to do was to step off this hamster wheel, escape from the Habitrail of life for at least one day to actually enjoy life.

We can live in the now and smell the proverbial roses, in other ways as well. At least once a month I devote my daily meditation time to reminding myself of all the things I have now, and what I should be appreciative of and thankful for: my health, her health, and the health of our dogs; the four walls and roof around us; our families; our friends; and a good job. When I finish the session, I get up and look around—and I mean *really look around*—at our home and all the things I should appreciate. All the things I can appreciate *now*.

You want to be a little more *"Zen"*? Well, Zen is about experiencing life in the here and now. Do this, and you are being Zen.

A famous Buddhist meditation is to contemplate the impermanence of your life, your health, your family, and your pets. We are all changing, all growing old. Our health will not last forever. Our pets, our family, and our friends will one day be gone, often before we even know it. We will all one day die, as Father Time is undefeated. The time to appreciate what we have in life is now—today; not only on the weekends; not until a distant future vacation; not only upon your retirement.

I often look at our beloved dogs and remind myself that every one of our human days is the equivalent of an entire week of their lives passing. This provides an extra impetus to spend quality time with them on a walk, playing fetch, or just giving them a good petting; and while I am doing so, to remind myself to enjoy and savior this time with them.

It is also funny, little things that can inspire me and us to be thankful for our health. A few months ago I passed by one of the staff in our hospital who told me with a big smile on his face:

Any day above the dirt is a good day.

He does not have the prestigious job I have. He does not have the financial resources I have. He does not drive a fancy car or have a big house. No, he has something far more valuable—an appreciation of life itself.

Each day alive is a gift. Switch off your mind's autopilot mode and take control of your awareness of each day and each moment. When you wake up in the morning, vow not to waste this day; vow to enjoy this day; vow to savor this day.

Remember the words of the Thai monk Ajahn Chah:

The days and nights
are passing relentlessly.
How well are we spending our time?

Let's make the most of our time. Now. Today.

Don't live in the yesterday.
Don't live in the tomorrow.
Live in the today.

How many people on their death bed say, "I wish I had lived my life differently," or "I wish I had appreciated it more?" Take five minutes and imagine that you are going to die soon. How would you live differently? What would you appreciate more?

Unless you absolutely believe in rebirth, reincarnation or heaven, and even if you do, it seems it is wise and advisable to make the most of every minute we have on earth, in this body we have been given. So stop mindlessly sleepwalking through life. Take back control of your mind and your life. Spend ten minutes meditating on (or just thinking about) the impermanence of everything we have—our health, our friends, our pets, our loved ones. Contemplate the inevitability and unpredictability of death itself. Then take a few minutes and take stock of all the good things in life you have right now, and vow to appreciate, enjoy, and savor it—right now, in this minute. When you wake up each morning, vow not to waste the day. Vow not to waste any day. And remind yourself:

> *I cannot change the past.*
> *I cannot predict the future.*
> *All I can do*
> *is appreciate the present.*

CHAPTER 11

WORRY

N othing can take control of your mind more insidiously than your worry submind, and your worry submind loves to worry. We worry, worry, worry. Worry, worry, worry. And then worry some more. Worry can ruin our day and turn blue skies gray. Surely, given our druthers, we would not choose to worry. We would not obsess over some possible future outcome, or worry about something in the past that we can no longer change. But our worry submind is a powerful one, embedded by evolution in our Pleistocene-era brain, when for the purposes of survival we had to be constantly concerned if a wild beast was around the next bend. Back then, worry was a critical survival mechanism. And it still has its place in our current era. Certainly, on a wet or icy roadway, we have to have an appropriate degree of concern and caution as we drive. And if we hear an intruder trying to break into our home, that's an appropriate cause of worry.

But in our current world, there are few truly life-threatening events that are legitimate causes of worry. Very few of the things we worry about in modern life represent clear and present dangers to our lives, our family, or our health. But as neuropsychology experts point out, our primitive, evolutionary worry proclivities now lead to endless maladaptive attitudes toward everyday life. In essence, our worry subminds have not learned to adapt to life in the twenty-first century.

Most of the things we worry about are, in the scheme of things, pretty superficial. What if whatever we are worrying about came true? Unless our worry concerns a dire health issue or life-threatening situation, we would not be dead. We would still have our health. We would still have our family and friends. We would still have a working brain. We would still have all of our limbs. Sure, there would likely be some setbacks, but in the scheme of our lives, how truly life-shaking and life-dooming would this be? It may be helpful to contemplate how superficial, at least in terms of life and death, most of our worries really are.

Further, the reality is that most of the things we worry about turn out to be nothing; they never materialize. And even when they do, the consequences are rarely as dire as our "worst case" worry submind anticipates.

An oft quoted saying, attributed to many but probably first spoken by Mark Twain, is

> *I have been through*
> *some terrible things in my life,*
> *some of which have actually*
> *happened.*

Think about it. How many things have you worried about that never came to fruition? I still remember a time when before I was about to become a cardiology fellow (the three years of training required to be a cardiologist). I had signed up to do a summer internship. For financial reasons though, I backed out of this months before it was to start. The internship director was quite upset with me and called the cardiology section chief, who then sent word that I was to meet with him. When I got a call that my future cardiology chief wanted to meet with me, I was filled with a sense of utter doom. My reputation would be in tatters, and my academic cardiology career would be over before it even started. For a week, I dreaded this day-of-reckoning with the chief, imagining case scenarios that grew worse by the day. When I finally did meet with him, what happened was a great big nothing. No scolding, no recriminations, nothing. I wish I had known back then what Mark Train had said, as it would have saved me a week of incredible anguish.

Another issue we tend to worry about is what others think or say about us. Like many of our other present-day worries, our insecurity and worry subminds amplify this concern way out of proportion to what is appropriate and what is actually true. One of the most helpful pearls of wisdom on this subject is in a book on Buddhist philosophy by *New York Times* best-selling author Robert Wright. He discusses worry, and more specifically how much we all worry about what others think of us. He recounts what his mother once told him:

> *We wouldn't spend so much time*
> *worrying about what others think of us*
> *if we realized how seldom they do.*

What an incredible insight. While we spend our days and nights worrying about what our friends, family, coworkers, or neighbors might be saying about us behind our back, in reality they are too busy living their own lives and dealing with their own problems to squander time gossiping about or maligning us.

When we worry, we should also mindfully contemplate what all this worrying is getting us. The answer is usually a big fat nothing. It does not solve the perceived problem nor ameliorate the situation. It does nothing helpful, and only serves to twist our mind into knots, to hijack whatever peace or happiness we could have in the present moment, and to adversely affect our physical health and well-being.

Joseph Goldstein observes:

> *It is helpful to reflect that worry*
> *has absolutely no bearing on outcome.*

The fact that worrying gains us nothing was recognized millennia ago in Matthew 6:27:

WORRY

Who among you by worrying
can add a single moment to your life?

It is also helpful to decide if you can or cannot do anything about what you are worrying about. I fly around the country (and in the past, internationally) a good amount, often with connecting flights. Not infrequently, the first flight will be delayed. If it is too delayed, I will miss my connection and have to spend the evening in God knows what town or flee-bag motel room, and possibly not get back to Houston for a busy scheduled day of hospital and clinic responsibilities. This seems an appropriate situation for rational concern. Yet, I try to remind myself, all the worrying in the world is not going to make whatever weather or mechanical problem get resolved one minute more quickly. I am powerless to affect the situation or change anything. So, rather than worry, I try to accept the situation—open up a book to read or go to the closest watering hole for a cold beverage.

When our worry subminds do start to shift into all-out panic mode, it's helpful to remind ourselves of what Robert Wright counsels:

> *Stop worrying about something*
> *you're powerless to influence*
> *(by your worrying).*

The Dalai Lama himself also suggests a similar approach:

> *It is more sensible to spend the energy*
> *focusing on the solution rather than*
> *worrying about the problem. . . .*
> *Alternately, if there is no way out, no*

solution, no possibility of resolution,
then there is also no point in being
worried about it, because you can't do
anything about it anyway.

He more pithily sums this up as follows:

If there is a solution to the problem,
there is no need to worry.
If there is no solution,
there is no sense in worrying either.

Another helpful strategy is the "glass is already broken" approach to worry. For instance, in my anecdote about missing my connecting flight, I find it helpful to sometimes accept ahead of time that it is likely that I will miss the flight. Once I accept this outcome, there is no longer anything to worry about, and I can begin dispassionately and rationally planning how I will deal with it (should it actually occur!).

Carrying around worry is like needlessly putting a lead weight in your briefcase, backpack, or purse that you carry around all day. Would you voluntarily carry a twenty-pound weight all day, wherever you go? Most likely not. But that is what we do when we let our worry submind overrun our conscious mind. How many unnecessary lead weights do you inadvertently carry around in your cranium each day? Put those lead weights down. Or better yet, don't pick them up in the first place.

We can take back control of our minds when we recognize that our Pleistocene era worry submind has shifted into hyperdrive. It has taken one of the innumerable occurrences or situations in everyday life, overinflated the seriousness of it, and caused us needless suffering about something that may not ever come true. Even if it does transpire, it is likely to be far less dire than we imagine—even though our worry submind loves to indulge itself in worst-case scenarios. We can remind ourselves that no matter how much we worry, we are incapable of influencing whether or not whatever we are worrying about will occur and what the outcome will be.

CHAPTER 12

MEDITATION 101

The importance and usefulness of meditation in understanding and thus controlling our minds and our lives has been recognized for literally thousands of years by numerous cultures and religions. There is no single better way to understand how your mind works, how your subminds strive to hijack your mind's thoughts and emotions, and how you can work to take back control of your mind, than through meditation. When you are meditating it is very easy to see when you are in control of your mind and when your subminds are in control.

As the Bengali Buddhist master and scholar Anagarika Munindra remarked half a century ago:

> *If you want to understand your mind,*
> *sit down and observe it.*

We spend much of our time thinking and worrying about external and physical phenomena: our bodies; our weight, our hair; our car; our house; our boyfriend; our job; and our finances. Yet, it is our internal environment—our thoughts, emotions, and mental attitude—that determines our happiness or unhappiness, our satisfaction with and appreciation of life, and how much inner peace we have or do not have. Shouldn't we then spend twenty minutes or so a day checking in with our mind, working to understand and retrain it, so we can take back control of it? This is meditation, and to get started is easier than you think.

We can boil down the steps of meditation to three things:

1. Find a quiet place to sit
2. Sit in whatever position is comfortable for you
3. Focus your mind on observing the breath—the in-breath and the out-breath

That's it! Congratulations—you are meditating!

Of course, there is more to it, but that is all you need to start meditating. In a future chapter, we will discuss the different types of meditation and more advanced practices, but let's not clutter up or confuse things for now.

While I'm neither an expert meditator nor professional meditation instructor, and this is not a book on meditation (and there are dozens of such great books – some of which I've listed in the appendix, as well as numerous podcasts and web-based guided meditations), I've been doing meditation for a while now. I've read a few dozen books on different methods and types of meditation, and experimented with meditation methods and variations. It may thus be useful to you if I share some of the lowdown on what you may read or hear about meditation and methods.

First, unless you plan to join a Zen monastery, don't worry about any specific way to sit, such as the particular way one sits cross legged in the "lotus position," as you may have read about or seen pictures of seemingly blissful advanced meditators in movies or magazines. There is no right way to sit. Simply find whatever sitting position is most comfortable for you.

That said, most people find it more comfortable if they sit on a pillow or meditation cushion, also known as a *zafu*, which raises your backside up and eases the strain on your back, particularly if sitting for more than just a few minutes. In addition to the cushion, I also like to have my entire body and the cushion on a rectangular padded floor mat called a *zabuton*, which makes it easier on my knees and feet. However, a folded blanket will work just as well.

When I first started meditating, I bought a nice, colorful matching cushion and padded floor mat. In addition to making the meditation more comfortable, it also provided some additional impetus to give this meditation stuff a real try, as I had just shelled out a hundred bucks for them. Plus, sitting on these ancient and Eastern accessories was just really cool! But I digress. Let me emphasize you do *not* need these items to start meditating!

If you have arthritis, knee, or back problems, and it is uncomfortable to sit on the floor, then sit upright in a chair. I have observed at meditation retreats that about a third of participants, as well as some instructors, seem to find it more comfortable to sit in a chair than sit on the floor. There is no shame or failure in doing so.

Same goes with where to place your hands when you are meditating. Don't get sidetracked or fixated about where you place your hands, or whether you hold them in some special type of position called a *mudra*. Just place them wherever and however it is most comfortable for *you*.

You can either close your eyes or keep them open a bit, and gently and softly gaze toward the floor a few feet in front of you. Having your eyes closed, particularly when you first start out, is probably easier, as it takes out of play any visual distractions. I personally meditate with my eyes open, as I feel it is more "real world" as far as my efforts to become more mindful in everyday life (I don't walk around with my eyes closed), but again this is strictly personal preference, and starting out with the eyes closed, as most people seem to do, is clearly easier.

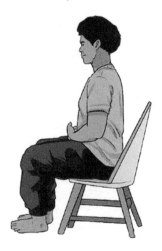

Next, there are numerous ways to observe or follow the breath, and you may read about numerous techniques or that only one is the "right way" to meditate. Again, don't drink the Kool-Aid. Find a practice that is best for you. Some will focus on the breath (really air) moving in and out of the nose and nostrils—though you may find this sensation too subtle to follow and difficult to keep your attention. Some will focus on the abdomen moving inward and outward—this is the "Zen way" to follow the breath. Some will find it easier to focus on the chest rising/expanding, then falling/deflating. Some may find it easier to focus on your body as a whole as it breathes in and out. I would suggest that you try several of these approaches, and see which one works best for you. Again, there is no right or wrong approach. The only caveat is to do whatever is best for you. The emphasis is on *following* or *observing* the breath, not consciously, actively breathing in an out (inhaling and exhaling) per se.

When you start, you will find that even simply following the breath can be challenging, and your mind will quickly start to wander. There are numerous techniques you can use to help you stay focused. You may quietly think to yourself *in-breath* each time you inhale, and *out-breath* each time you exhale (or just think *in* and then *out*). You may count the breaths, seeing if you can do this counting up to five or ten breaths in a row without losing focus, then repeating this again and again. To keep your mind more interested and focused, you may begin to break down each breath in a little more detail, other than just in or out. Particularly as you start to train your mind to better focus, you will notice that there are multiple distinct phases of each breath (e.g., initial, continuing, and ending stages), as well as a brief pause once you have finished exhaling, before you begin to inhale again. You may notice that different parts of your abdomen, chest wall, lungs, and even shoulders expand or rise, then fall or deflate, at different stages of the inhalation and exhalation. You can read more about these techniques and tricks in numerous books and podcasts on meditation. Again, find what works best for *you*.

When you first start meditating, it may be best to try it for just five or ten minutes at a time, each day, for the first week or two. This will keep you interested and help keep you from becoming discouraged. Over time, you can gradually increase the amount of time you spend meditating. From what I have read, heard, and experienced, a reasonable and realistic goal may be to work up to twenty to forty-five minutes a day, but see what works best for you, and what best fits your schedule. Regardless of the time you spend in meditation, everyone agrees that it is best to try to meditate every day (or at least most days of the week), rather than just once every now and then. When you jog, work out, or use free weights every day (or at least three to four times a week), you and your body build up your muscles and your endurance. This is same with meditation. Your mental abilities to focus and stay focused grow much better with a daily practice than just the random once a week, or once a month, sit down.

Within minutes (or even seconds) of your first attempt at meditation, you will undoubtedly notice that try as you might, your mind starts to wander and random thoughts keep popping into your head. You may think to yourself that you are "not doing it right," "can't do it," or "are a failure." Please note that this happens to everyone, even people who have been meditating for years. Let me repeat this critical point so that you do not become discouraged: *this happens to everyone*. It's normal. Remember, *thoughts think themselves*, or your subminds think these thoughts. While you may want to focus on the breath, your subminds have their own agenda and are always looking for opportunities to impart their desires, worries, memories, cravings, fears, anxieties, and regrets into your consciousness. Recognizing that you, try as you might, cannot control your mind nor prevent the occurrence of seemingly random thoughts popping into it is, in itself, a huge insight and accomplishment. This is one of the first, and one of the most important, lessons we get from beginning a meditation practice.

Recognizing *when* your mind starts to wander is a second huge achievement. This means you are now beginning to develop *awareness* and *mindfulness*. You are beginning to recognize when you are controlling your mind, and when you are not. You are beginning to develop awareness of what is happening with your thoughts in the present moment. This is mindfulness. You are beginning to develop mindfulness! At first, your mind may wander for minutes at a time before you recognize it is wandering. Over time (weeks, months, years), the time your mind wanders before you recognize this will decrease. This is growing mindfulness.

So when your mind starts to wander, and it will—again and again—just recognize this, congratulate yourself on your awareness of it, and refocus on following the breath or counting the breaths. You are not failing. You are succeeding. This is meditation.

Again, don't be discouraged! If you go to a meditation class or retreat, it may seem to you that everyone else is "doing it right" and are seemingly deep in a perfect stage of flawlessly following the breath (or being present "in the moment"). I guarantee you they are not. Just like you, they are struggling. Just like you, their minds are wandering. Just like you, random thoughts are popping into their head. It was a revelation to me at one meditation retreat when one of the instructors asked the participants to raise their hands if they were struggling with the aches and pains of sitting or trying to stay focused, and almost all hands went up.

Let's address a few more important caveats to meditation as you begin to develop a practice. When you meditate, you will not be perfect at it, but you *will* ultimately become better and better, and that is more than OK. In fact, that is the goal. Practicing free throw shooting does not result in you never missing a free throw, but with practice you will make more shots. Practicing a gymnastics move doesn't mean you will always do it perfectly, but you will do it better. The same applies to meditation. Unless you go full "shaved head" and become a robed monk for years and years, you will never eliminate the occasional thoughts that randomly pop into your head, but you will gradually get better at staying focused for longer periods of time—perhaps a few minutes at a time instead of just a few seconds.

Second, like many other things, your meditation skills will *gradually* improve. Don't expect to be great, or even good, when you first start. When you start weight-lifting training, you do not, and cannot, start out with 300 pounds of weight on the bench press. You start out with modest weights, and as your muscles strengthen, you add more weight every few weeks. Same with jogging. You don't start out trying to go from a couch potato to a marathon runner on the first day hitting the pavement. It is a gradual process.

Third, meditation is an *active* process. It is not zoning out, but tuning in. You don't just sit on a cushion and veg out. It is mental work (and remember, the brain uses twenty-five percent of all the oxygen consumed by the body). You have to actively focus on the breath, not passively sit there or space out. When you are not at least trying to focus, you are not meditating. John Yates calls this vegging out or spacing out of the brain "dullness"—a term I like and that helped me to catch myself spacing out. You don't get stronger, or develop greater endurance, when you go to the gym or fitness center and just sit on an exercise bike or stand motionless on the treadmill. You have to engage, just as you must actively engage your mind. As innumerable instructors have remarked, it is not called meditation *practice* for nothing.

Finally, as you meditate, take the time to enjoy it. This is *your* time to devote five, ten, or twenty minutes just to you. Turn away from the endless thoughts, worries, concerns, obligations, and tasks of the future. Just be with yourself. This is your twenty minutes of designated "me time" that you are entitled to take once a day. This is your time to just be. As your mind starts to relax, as you begin to take back control of your mind, you will find this to be a wonderful and peaceful feeling. Feel it; enjoy it; and savor this time.

The primary purposes of meditation are long term: to improve your ability to focus and control your mind; to gain insight on how your mind works; and to become more mindful. But, as an added carrot to trying meditation, I will also tell you that there is an immediate short term benefit each day as well. Our minds are constantly cluttered with worries, concerns, and anxieties about what has happened in the past and what might happen in the future. We are planning for things we need to accomplish today and what we need to do this weekend. We are worried about a family member's health, the bills, the leaky toilet. Taking a ten or twenty-minute pause each day to meditate can reboot your brain. It's as if there are fifteen different "programs" open at once in your brain, and your computer brain just doesn't have enough RAM (memory) to deal with all of these at the same time, resulting in inefficient thinking or thought processing, and a "freezing up" of its functioning. Meditation is like turning off your computer and then rebooting it. It allows you to start the day, or the rest of the day, fresh and refreshed.

So, what do you say? Ready to give it a try? While I cannot speak for everyone, I can tell you that a daily (or mostly daily) meditation practice has been transformative in my life. I was not a tree hugging, flower power, touchy-feely, granola crunching, hippy-type person who was a natural fit for meditation. I was instead a hard-working, left-brained, type A individual, just like many of you, who never gave a thought to something as esoteric as meditation. But it's pretty cool to do once you get the hang of it, and it really works. Just as it's done for me, it will make you appreciate life more and be a better person. And it will help you to understand and to ultimately start taking control of your mind. So I encourage you to try it, at least for a few weeks, and see how it changes your life.

CHAPTER 13

DON'T SLEEPWALK
THROUGH LIFE

Although we all may feel like we are consciously choosing to do what we do each and every minute, hour, day, and year, and that we are aware of and savoring each and every moment we are not six feet under or ashes in an urn, this is probably not the case. Life, and all our responsibilities, obligations, and commitments, has a way of washing us along, day after day after day, until the days become weeks, the weeks become months, the months become years, the years become decades, and then we die. Unless we really pause to consider where we are, who we are with, and what we are doing, we run the risk of sleepwalking through life; of simply floating down the proverbial river of life, carried by the current, and powerless to navigate our own course or see where we are going, or where we want to go.

Have you ever observed an anthill, with its hundreds of worker ants mindlessly performing their genetically pre-programmed repetitive jobs, hour after hour, day after day? Are we so different from these ants, doing the same

nine to five, day after day? Worker ants never question why they're doing what they're doing; whether or not they're happy doing it; and whether they have any other options in their life. In ant society, the worker ant is applauded for bringing back a big piece of whatever it is that they bring back to the anthill. The ant is applauded, that is, until it has worked itself so hard and so long that it is enfeebled and no longer useful to the colony. It is the same in our society. We applaud those who work themselves to the bone, put in long hours every day and on weekends, take working vacations, and have risen to the rank of store manager or company VP, only to have worked their life away until they no longer have a chance to enjoy what little there is left of it. In the song "Ants Marching" by the Dave Mathews Band are the lyrics " . . .all the little ants are marching." We are those ants.

Sometimes, we may feel like a hamster stuck in a Habitrail, where all those plastic tubes are connected together, channeling the poor rodent to where it can go, and preventing it from going where it truly wants to go. Only in our lives there are not plastic tubes but rather roads and subways, which we travail back and forth on to our jobs, day after day after day. Sometimes, instead of a subway, we may feel like we're stuck on a bullet train, with life and events propelling us forward and out of our control.

Our minds have been programmed to autopilot, and the software that has been loaded into it by our subminds, and by society, is to work, work, work and to acquire more, more, more, without ever pausing to ponder what we are doing and why we are doing it, nor stopping to appreciate the present moment. We are sleepwalking through life: wake, shower, work, sleep. Wake, shower, work, sleep. Wake, shower, work, sleep. It may be worthwhile to occasionally pause and ask yourself:

> *How many times in life are you deciding where to go, and how many times is life deciding for you where you will go?*

In order to take control of our minds, and our lives, perhaps it is useful to step off the assembly line, or conveyer belt, of life and sit and ponder for an hour, day, or week, where we are in life, and what we are doing day after day. Think about what we *really* want in life. Ponder if we, ourselves, are navigating our future, or are we instead being washed down the stream by life by events we don't control, or bother to control, and just passively flow wherever the current takes us. Doesn't it make sense to wade out of the river and sit on the bank for a while?

We must also try, as best we can, to actively enjoy life. To appreciate the moment. To awaken from our reflexive and preprogrammed habit of "going through the motions" and instead focus on savoring the journey. Miley Cyrus's song "The Climb" underscores this point about reaching the mountain top:

> *Ain't about how fast I get there.*
> *Ain't about what's waiting*
> *on the other side.*
> *It's the climb.*

So pause every now and then as you climb the mountain to appreciate the view.

An equally important message comes from the Tim McGraw song "Live Like You Were Dying," which is about a man in his 40s diagnosed with a fatal disease. It is then, and only then, he goes out and truly enjoys life, becomes a better husband and a better person. The catch line of the song goes:

> *Someday I hope you get the chance*
> *to live like you were dying.*

Let's hope we do not need a fatal diagnosis to stop sleep-walking through life and instead wake up to the little joys of everyday life and to the gift of life itself. I certainly would not choose to have cancer, but I often wonder if those who survive cancer have a greater appreciation of life and the preciousness of each day than those of us who slog through life day to day, oblivious to the fact that the months in our calendar of life are quickly peeling away and falling to the ground, never to be reclaimed or relived.

So let's every now and then mindfully take a pause from being swept passively down the river of life and consider if we are just sleepwalking through life, or truly navigating our own path and living life. Let's vow, as much as we can, to set our own course, with the following guidance:

Don't sleepwalk through life.
Appreciate Life.
Enjoy Life.
Savor Life.
Live life.

CHAPTER 14

RIDE THE WAVES

What we all want is to be blissfully out on our sailboat with sunny skies, perfect weather, and calm seas. But inevitably, rough waves sometimes occur and disrupt our tranquility. These waves crash down upon us, disrupt our peace, or even try to knock us out of our comfort zone and into the blustery water. These waves are an inevitable part of life.

The waves of life can be as simple as a traffic jam, the home AC breaking down, or a girlfriend wanting to do something different from what you planned, to the more serious events of a loved one's illness (or a pet's), the house flooding, or the loss of a job.

These waves, big and small, come at us every day. There's no stopping them. The key though, is how we deal with them. Do we take them in stride, as the price of doing business—and the "business" is being alive—or do we rail, curse, and revile them, allowing them and our reaction to take over our thoughts, our emotions, our reactions, and our mind? As we discussed, we do have a choice, and the choice is up to us. It's up to us decide how we are going to react to the turbulent waves of life.

Like you, in the various positions of responsibility I've had in my professional and personal life, waves arise every day that I must deal with. In my various leadership roles in the hospital where I work, I can get hit at any time with a tsunami of waves—endless bureaucracy, unmeetable performance measures, staffing issues, personality challenges, scheduling issues, blah, blah, blah. To remind myself of the skillful way to handle these occurrences, I have put front and center on my desk a picture of crashing waves, and the following strategy I crafted for myself:

> *Expect the waves.*
> *Recognize the waves.*
> *Accept the waves.*
> *Ride the waves.*
> *Then let them pass.*

Waves are going to come—every single day. I need to expect and accept that in these positions of responsibility this is going to happen. When they do come, I need to be able to recognize that one of these waves is hitting me now. I need to accept that it is yet another one of life's challenges, and that I have been hired to deal with the situation as best I can, just as we all have to deal with running a household, raising a family, or being a worthy partner in a relationship. I need to avoid getting swamped or swept away figuratively by them into a maelstrom of negative emotions and instantaneous, unthoughtful reactions.

Once I can recognize and accept the situation, I can then hopefully pause and mindfully, skillfully step back and

Expect the wave
Recognize the wave
Accept the wave
Ride the wave
Then let it pass

assess how best to respond, rather than react thoughtlessly. Finally, once I have dealt with the waves, I need to let them pass, rather than perseverate about the issues, bring them home, and ruin my night or weekend.

In Jon Kabat-Zinn's famous book *Wherever You Go, There You Are* (a "must read" for those interested in mindfulness and an Eastern approach to living a better, happier life), he describes a poster of a Buddhist elder riding a surfboard in a wave-filled ocean. The caption on the poster reads:

> *You can't stop the waves,*
> *but you can learn to surf.*

Nothing sums up better the problems and frustrations—or inevitable "waves"—that we will face every day, and how we must skillfully approach them.

We all have our daily waves in life that come at us, whatever our age, gender, job, family structure, physical appearance, or social relationships. They test our true metal—what we are made of, our inner strength to deal with hardship, and how "adult" we really are.

These waves of adversity, as the saying goes, build character. As Franklin Delano Roosevelt, a man paralyzed by polio yet who served during the great depression and World War II as one of our greatest presidents, remarked:

> *A smooth sea*
> *never made a skilled sailor.*

Author Richard Carlson suggests we remind ourselves of the following:

> *Life is rarely the way we want it to be.*

It can't and won't always be calm seas and smooth sailing. So when your *impatience submind* gets upset that the table you reserved is not yet ready and tries to put you in a bad mood, ruining an otherwise delightful evening out, take back control of your mind and remind yourself of this, and just ride the wave. When your child knocks over the glass of grape juice onto the living room carpet, ride the wave. When your flight is delayed, ride the wave. When your partner or family decide to change the plans you've made, ride the wave.

Recognizing in the moment when we are getting hit with one of the many waves of life is not easy. It takes practice. Remaining calm and level-headed is easy when everything is going well and the river is calm. But it is during times of adversity, when we suddenly find ourselves in the rapids, that require us to have equanimity, and to take control of our thoughts, emotions, reactions, and actions. To remind myself of this, I will occasionally reread the poem on the following page, which I wrote (I promise you is the only poem my left-sided brain will ever write).

When the Rapids Appear

It is easy
to go with the flow
when the river is calm and clear.

But what tests
equanimity though,
is when rapids now appear.

We cannot deal
with the rapids in life,
lest we first recognize when they are here.

Then mindfully,
with this recognition of strife,
with equanimity must we steer.

See if you can spend one day identifying, in real-time, the waves that come at you. And see how well you can navigate the waves and rapids of life.

CHAPTER 15

STRESS

S tress is the evil stepchild of worry. It permeates our modern culture and society. When the American Psychological Association conducted its annual survey on stress in 2011, nearly a quarter of respondents reported their levels of stress as "extreme." Thirty-nine percent said their stress had gone up in the past year, and forty-four percent said it had increased in the past five years. More recently, in a 2018 Gallup poll, more than half (fifty-five percent) of Americans reported experiencing stress during "a lot of the day" prior. But what exactly is stress, and where does it come from?

If you google the definition of stress, you'll find "a state of mental or emotional strain or tension resulting from adverse or very demanding circumstances." But this is not correct. Stress is what results from our mind's, or worry submind's, *perception of* and *reaction to* external circumstances or events. This is a subtle but critical point. External circumstances, in themselves, cannot cause stress. They are just events, occurrences, phenomena. In themselves, they have no power to mystically cause stress to ourselves. It is how we *choose* to react to these external circumstances that can either lead, or not lead, to our sensation of stress.

As Andrew Bernstein, author of *The Myth of Stress*, writes:

> *The truth is that stress doesn't come from your boss, your kids, your spouse, traffic jams, health challenges, or other circumstances. It comes from your thoughts about these circumstances.*

This point cannot be emphasized enough. In any situation, we can control how we react—or not react—to something. Jon Kabat-Zinn, the father of *mindfulness-based stress reduction*, observes:

> *It is not the potential stressor itself, but how you perceive it and then how you handle it, that will determine whether or not it will lead to stress.*

Similarly, Chris Prentiss, in his book *Zen and the Art of Happiness*, emphasizes that stress comes from the way you relate to events or situations. To paraphrase him:

> *Things are just things,*
> *events merely events,*
> *situations only situations.*
> *It is up to you to supply*
> *your reaction to them.*
> *YOU get to choose.*

It may be helpful to visualize that in your Pleistocene-era stress submind is a fire that erupts from time to time. The initial flame that flares up within you may be understandable and even biologically advantageous (say, for example, if you see a poisonous snake that's about to strike you). But imagine a little man or woman in your stress submind who keeps shoveling coals into that fire, causing it to grow and burn even stronger. *Stress submind Sparky,* as we will call him, does not realize that whatever has caused the initial stress response has passed. Stress submind Sparky continues to overreact to the situation. He can think of nothing else and just keeps feeding the fire. This is your stress submind in overdrive. When we recognize this state, we can take the shovel out of the hands of Sparky, send him away, and allow the fire to die out. Better yet, envision throwing a bucket of water on the fire and extinguishing it right then and there. Try to picture the now extinguished fire. If and when, during the day, the fire starts to smolder again in your stress submind, recognize it, shoo away stress submind Sparky, and forge ahead.

Stress Submind Sparky

How can we take this shovel out of the hands of stress submind Sparky? One strategy is to put the perceived stressful event or issue in perspective. As the saying goes:

Life is not an emergency.

The problem is, a mind taken over by stress may think just that—that everything *is* a true emergency. Natalie Goldberg, a new age author and speaker, notes that

> *Stress is an ignorant state.*
> *It believes that everything*
> *is an emergency.*

We need to distinguish between the truly life-threatening or life-changing events we will face in our lifetime from the innumerable, inevitable, non-life-threatening issues that come up in our daily lives. These are things, often unpleasant or frustrating, we must deal with, but they are not emergencies.

A Persian proverb helps put things in perspective:

> *I complained I had no shoes,*
> *until I met a man who had no feet!*

We may not get that raise; the person we met on a blind date may not call us back or respond to our text messages; we may not get that assignment in on time; or we're already late and traffic is backed up. None of these are desirable situations, and many circumstances in life are appropriately concerning. But how many are more like "having no shoes," and how many are more like "having no feet?"

Dean Smith, the late legendary North Carolina basketball coach, no doubt dealt with a lot of pressure-filled situations in his lifetime. But he seemed to have kept things in perspective, judging by his saying that

If you treat every situation
as a life and death matter,
you'll die a lot of times.

To help keep things in perspective, in situations of perceived stress, we can ask ourselves:

Will this matter a year from now?
Will I even remember this
a year from now?
Will this matter on my deathbed?

We can use the mindfulness RAIN (or RAID) approach to stress. As you may remember, we first mindfully **R**ecognize that stress is occurring. This is an important and very mindful step in and of itself. We can't just fight this feeling or magically turn it off, but rather our second step is to **A**ccept that stress is present. Third, we calmly and dispassionately **I**nvestigate what truly is leading us to react with this feeling of stress. What is actually causing, or leading to, a sensation of stress (e.g., fear of failure, fear of embarrassment)? Is our worry really appropriate? Is it proportional to whatever may happen, even if what happens is the worst-case scenario (e.g., being late to a meeting, missing a deadline)? Fourth, we **D**e-identify with the stress. We note its presence and view it as a formless, massless phenomena extrinsic to

113

ourselves. We hold it in our hands, and keep it at arms' length from our minds.

Alternatively, we can visualize the stress as a hot coal that we metaphysically move out of our focus and put into an insulative ceramic bowl, situated in the far corner of our consciousness. We can then let it slowly burn itself out, as it inevitably will. It may take minutes. It may take hours. But like every emotion we experience, it will inevitably go out.

Stress can also result from feeling overwhelmed, a perception that there are just too many things to do. In the abstract, our mind cannot deal with five or ten vague, ill-defined concepts about things we need to do, how to prioritize them, and where to start. I have found it very helpful in such times to write down on a three-by-five-inch index card, or piece of paper, a list of all the tasks I must accomplish with a little box next to each task. This serves to break down the abstract concept of overwhelming tasks, which my stress submind loves to obsess over, into bite-size chunks of achievable tasks. Rather than feeling paralyzed by a seemingly impossible mission, I can get started on task number one, and when completed check it off the list and move on to task number two. This simple exercise "takes the ball" out of the hands of my stress submind, and allows me to rationally and systematically take back control of my mind, setting about addressing one-by-one what was previously an overwhelming and stress-provoking amalgam of tasks and responsibilities. It is remarkable how this simple exercise leads to the dissolution of the stressful feeling of being overwhelmed.

David Allen, the author of *Getting Things Done*, has observed:

*Much of the stress that people feel
doesn't come from having too much
to do.
It comes from not finishing what
they've started.*

Breaking down the tasks at hand, whether they be written on an index card or in some other manner, and then starting and finishing each task systematically, allows you to solve the problem, rather than stress about it.

There are many other strategies for dealing with feelings of overwhelm. The common theme in these strategies is to first recognize when these stressed-out feelings boil up from your stress submind and take over your thoughts and emotions. Then you can implement any one of these strategies to actively take back control of your mind and begin to regain a sense of balance and ease.

CHAPTER 16

ENOUGH

I n the 1980s movie *Arthur*, the late actor Dudley Moore, playing a wealthy but childish man searching for himself, is sitting at a bar, midday. He has clearly had more than his share of hard alcohol already, but asks the bartender for another drink. The bartender looks him over and tells him that it looks like "You have had enough." Arthur replies "I want more than enough." In an era before the dangers and consequences of alcoholism and drunk driving had been fully appreciated, the line was funny at the time. But taken more metaphorically, it serves as a reminder of our own self-destructive and self-defeating attitudes as we go about our lives.

Our hedonism, pleasure, envy, avarice, and gluttony subminds all want more, more, more. More wealth, more possessions, more power, more sex, more stuff. They crave a bigger house, fancier car, and more bling. These subminds are never satisfied or satiated, and lead us to not appreciate, nor be content with, what we already have.

If we have a Toyota, we want a Lexus. If we have a Lexus, we want a Mercedes. If we have a Mercedes, we want a Bentley. If we have a nice sports car with 250 horse-power that can go from zero to sixty in seven seconds, we still crave our neighbor's sports car that is 350 horsepower and can go from zero to sixty in six seconds. If we have a flat screen TV, we want a bigger flat screen TV. If we have an HDTV, we want a 4K TV. If we book a vacation at a nice three-star hotel that provides all we need, we neverthe-less fantasize about staying at a five-star hotel that Brad, Britney, George, Angelina, Justin, Taylor, and Kim stay at. We have more than enough shoes (or in my case cowboy boots) to wear each day, but still crave yet just another pair.

Let me give you one personal example of this. We have a good-sized brick house, adjacent to a golf course, with a pool and yard for our dogs to play in. It's more than big enough for Lydia, me, and our three dogs. It's in a nice neighborhood, with good neighbors. The air conditioner and heater both work, and the roof doesn't leak, providing us with a more than comfortable and safe shelter. In short, it is *enough*. But every now and again, as we are mind-lessly watching TV shows that feature mansions for sale in Beverly Hills, houses of the rich and famous, oceanfront villas, or homes with million dollar pools and backyards, I catch myself wanting to have enough money to live in one of those fantasy homes. I realize that I—at that moment—am not content with enough, but am wanting *more than enough*.

Envy is the green monster that lives in our skull. To para-phrase from the website Quizlet, envy is defined as "a feel-ing of discontent or resentful longing aroused by someone else's possessions, qualities, or achievements." Gluttony is one of the seven deadly sins and is a limitless and insa-tiable appetite leading to overindulgence. A definition of hedonism is "regarding pleasure, above all else, as the chief goal in life." None of this sounds like a recipe for happiness and inner peace or for being a good person or parent. And all of these cravings, at any moment, are waiting 24/7/365 to take control of our otherwise content mind and throw it into states of desire, disarray, despair, disappointment, dejection, and depression.

Thich Nhat Hanh makes the following observation, which sums up life in twenty-first century Western culture:

> We have a habit of running after things.
> We don't feel fulfilled in the here and
> now, so we run after all kinds of things
> we think will make us happier.
> We sacrifice our life chasing after objects.
> We chase after our life's dreams,
> and yet lose ourselves along the way.

We forget, or never even see, that most of the world does not have enough. There are tens of millions of people dying of hunger every year because they don't have even one basic meal a day. These are the homeless people throughout the world as well as in our own communities. Entire villages and populations perish from dehydration from a simple lack of drinkable water. The millions suffering with, and dying from, completely preventable diseases because they don't have access to basic health care, vaccines, or even antibiotics. We lose complete perspective of what is enough, and what is more than enough.

As Timber Hawkeye noted:

> Instead of being grateful for what we
> already have, we exhaust ourselves

with cravings and longings for what
we haven't yet attained.

Clearly, this is not a prescription for a happy life. In order to take back control of our lives, we need to set some quiet time aside to sit, ponder, and remind ourselves of all the things we have and should be grateful for. We need to take stock of the fact that what we have is enough. And we need to evaluate when what we are often craving is more than enough. If having more than enough is okay with you (and, full disclosure, I have more than enough of many things), then perhaps consider what is *way more* than enough.

I'm not making a utopian argument that a better job, a nicer house, or any material possession is intrinsically wrong. But we should not crave these things nor base an assessment of our lives on the size of our house, the speed of our car, or the price of our shoes.

As Sheryl Crow so aptly sang in her song "Soak up the Sun":

> *It's not having what you want,*
> *It's wanting what you've got.*

In discussing true wealth, Thai forest monk Ajahn Chah remarked:

> *When we think of treasure, we only*
> *think of things such as money, posses-*
> *sions, jewels and gold. We don't con-*
> *sider our own eyes, ears, nose, organs,*
> *limbs and body. How much is your*

eyesight worth? How much would
you pay for a limb?

True wealth is not the size of our apartment or house, how sparkly our watch is, the brand name stitched on the butt of our jeans, or the size of our IRA or SEP. True wealth is not a Rolex or a Louis Vuitton handbag. True wealth is our health, our friends, and our family. How much money would you ask for in return for your eyes and vision? How much would you sell your legs for? Hundreds of thousands of dollars? Millions of dollars? Many of us would likely respond that we would not sell these for any amount of money; that they are priceless. Get the picture?

We cannot take back control of our minds if our hedonism, envy, and gluttony subminds are always screaming out unchecked for more, more, more. We must become able to recognize, them tame and quench these insatiable desires. We have to learn to become adept at discerning the difference between appreciating something and craving something. So please, take ten minutes to sit and contemplate how much you already have, and how rich your life already is. Ponder what is enough and what is more than enough.

CHAPTER 17

LET IT GO

Wouldn't it be great if there was one strategy in life to avoid all frustration, annoyance, aggravation, and anger, while remaining in a state of blissful happiness? And wouldn't it be great if you did not need to spend years in therapy or meditating in a monastery to learn this strategy? And even better, what if it were free, and you could start today?

The good news: there is such a strategy and approach to life. And this strategy can be described in three short words:

Let it go.

"Huh?" you might mutter dismissively. Pure and utter gibberish! Nothing is that simple! I can't believe I blew ten bucks on this book for that mindless new-age dripple!

But let me explain. Let's go to the common anecdote that you are happily driving along, perhaps to meet a date, visit relatives, or some other happy occasion. Someone zooms past you, driving way too fast on your left, then, without signaling, swerves into your lane, cutting you off

and forcing you to hit the brakes. Maybe they were mad because they thought you were driving too slowly. To add insult to injury, they flip you the bird and zoom ahead out of view, leaving you to literally eat their dust. Your initial reaction might have been surprise or even fear, but that quickly passes. You could forget the event, and return to your state of anticipation and happiness. But your subminds won't let that happen. Your ego, pride, and machismo subminds are filled with indignation at this person who cut you off. The more your submind stews over this act of disrespect, the angrier and more activated it becomes in your mind. It takes over your thoughts and before you know it, you are filled with umbrage, anger, and perhaps rage. You think of speeding up, just to try to catch this nefarious driver and flip them the bird right back. Maybe even cut the moron off or run the jerk off the road.

Surely, you would not opt to spend the next hour enraged, replaying the episode in your head, and plotting what you might do the next time some yahoo cuts you off. But that's exactly what you do. You are not controlling your mind. Instead your offended and angered ego (or machismo or pride) submind is in charge. What is the antidote to this scenario? To *let it go* or, as New Yorkers might say, *"fuhgeddaboudit!"*

The simple act of letting go is you reasserting control over your mind, deciding that peacefulness and happiness is more important to you than revenge, retribution, or whatever other negative thoughts you're entertaining.

The monk Ajahn Chah had perhaps the most profound insight into the strategy of letting go, and how this can lead to uninterrupted peace and happiness:

> *If you let go a little,*
> *this will lead to a little peace.*
> *If you let go a lot,*
> *this will lead to a lot of peace.*
> *If you let go completely,*
> *this will lead to complete peace.*

Have you ever see an unhappy or mad Australian? Probably not. Why? Because what are Australians famous for saying?

No worries.

I love Australians for their tolerant, laid-back approach to life. 'No worries' is their motto for just letting go.

Joseph Goldstein brilliantly uses a TV remote control as a metaphor for letting go of situations that make us upset. He points out that "we have an 'inner remote control' with the ability to change channels." The remote control is us, taking back control of our mind from the submind that continues to fixate on a perceived slight by our boss, an argument with our boyfriend, or an altercation with a grumpy neighbor. Instead, change the channel of our focus to the present, by perhaps refocusing on something pleasant that is occurring at that very moment. So the next time something small upsets you in the scheme of life, change the channel.

Another strategy for letting go is to put whatever has set you off in perspective. Ask yourself the questions: Will this really matter a year from now? Will this matter when I'm dying or dead? The answer is almost always no. So what seems like such a big deal in the moment really isn't in the bigger scheme of life.

Such a strategy is brilliantly summed up by the title of psychotherapist Richard Carlson's bestselling book:

Don't Sweat the Small Stuff . . .
and it's all small stuff

This phrase (which Carlson attributes to motivational speaker Wayne Dyer but may have been coined by author Robert Eliot) can serve as a blueprint or roadmap for letting go of probably ninety percent of all unpleasant occurrences in daily life.

Throughout my earlier life, I had the character flaw of tending to believe and expect that everyone should do everything as good and as fast as I (at least in my mind!). I had little patience for those who did things too slowly, poorly, or not at all. This was a recipe for endless frustration. Some examples of the little things that would pull my strings and push my buttons included:

- People not responding to emails;
- Colleagues and coworkers who showed up late for my meetings or missing deadlines;

- The driver in front of me who stopped at a green light and can't decide whether to turn right, go straight, or just sit there until the light turns red (or they finished texting);
- The internet (or phone or satellite TV) provider's so-called "help line" that put me on endless hold, then dropped my call; and
- The cashier at the drive-through who gave me sugar-laden Coke instead of the Diet Coke I ordered.

At the end of the day though, these annoyances all fall into the category of "small stuff." They are things that will not matter a year from now and they are things that, no matter how frustrated I become, I cannot change. So really, why become frustrated, upset, or angry over them? Just as worrying will not change the ultimate outcome of a situation, neither will becoming frustrated or upset. Just accept them as the uncontrollable hiccups, speed bumps, and inevitable waves of life we must surf. It's an all-around better approach to take control of one's mind and consciously decide to just go with the flow.

The Serenity Prayer, reportedly written by the American theologian Reinhold Niebuhr, offers us another strategy for letting go. There are many versions of this prayer, one of which is:

> *Change the things that can be changed,*
> *accept those that cannot,*
> *and have the wisdom to know*
> *the difference.*

We must also learn to be able to let go of our plans. When my family gets together, it often falls upon me to try to "herd the cats" and figure out when and where we will go out to eat or spend the day. On occasion, the plan I'd spent hours researching and getting buy-in from all parties, and which I was looking forward to, changes at the last minute. Someone wants to do something else. Someone doesn't like seafood. Someone doesn't want to spend the afternoon outside, all day, on a boat. Someone doesn't like that restaurant. This brings me to the proverbial crossroads of either becoming upset about this change in plans, or just going with the flow. I can recount in my life endless such examples, as I am sure you can as well. Over the years, through reading, meditating, and reflecting, I have become better at dealing with such situations. In fact, as I mentioned in the book's preface, several years ago, after I had started my transformative journey, my then 80-year-old mother, noting that I was a lot calmer and more even-tempered, gave me the backhanded compliment by telling me something along the lines of "You're a much better person than you used to be."

A strategy that the new, or at least a little more enlightened me tries to use, is one by Richard Carlson, who counsels us to

> *Expect that a certain percentage of plans will change.*

Along these same lines, Jon Kabat-Zinn advises us to

> *Avoid the trap of thinking 'I've got to have conditions be just so in order for the moment to be a happy moment.'*

Believing things must be "just so" to be happy is a sure way to be wind up unhappy, as you will invariably be frustrated and disconcerted when they are not so—which is probably the case for most of the events in our lives.

Ed Halliwell, a mindfulness teacher and co-author of the book *Mindfulness*, suggests the following:

> *Rather than always trying to do*
> *something about what's going on,*
> *practice being with it.*

We do not need to always "fix" something or some situation. We can just be in the moment and go with the flow.

So, getting back to my family get-togethers, as these wise sages counsel, if plans change, the skillful strategy for me is to sit back, accept it, go with the new plan (because plans inevitably change), and enjoy the time we have together—at whatever restaurant.

In these situations, I try to remind myself of the following question: what is more important, getting what I want and keeping my plans or going with the flow? Is it really that important we go out to eat at restaurant X or spend the day on a boat, or is it more important we accommodate the needs, desires, or wishes of family members, as best as the situation allows? This strategy has served me well in recent years—and impressed my mother!

Letting go is not surrendering. Letting go is not being passive. It is just the opposite. It is seizing back control of your mind from your stubborn, self-centered, short-sighted ego, pride, and craving subminds and making a thoughtful, skillful, and active decision for both your happiness and the happiness of others to move on, or go with the flow, than cling to your desire or plan. To paraphrase Noah Rasheta, a secular Buddhist teacher:

> *Letting go is not a sacrifice,*
> *but rather an act of liberation.*

Letting go liberates you from the negativity associated with clinging to a desire, conviction, or craving. Buddha is reported to have said:

> *You can only lose what you cling to.*

If we are not obsessed with proving ourselves right during an argument or attached to our desires or a particular outcome, we can let go and avoid conflict, remorse, disappointment, and irritation. We can avoid all the negativity that comes with losing something and not getting our way.

This is not to say there are not issues in life worth fighting for. Some are critical to our and our family's survival and prosperity. Some things our moral values simply do not allow us to accede to. In these cases, it is incumbent upon us to stand firm. But such things are likely only a small minority of the endless occurrences and situations we deal with in our daily lives. With mindfulness, skillfulness, and the goal of taking back control of our minds, we can pause and ask ourselves: Is this a situation of such magnitude, importance, or moral belief that I should stand my ground, or does this fall into the category of small stuff, where it is better to let it go?

CHAPTER 18

IS IT USEFUL?

I n his book *10% Happier,* Dan Harris recalled hearing
Joseph Goldstein, at a meditation retreat, urge the audience before doing something to first ask themselves the
following question:

Is it useful?

Though I initially glossed over this anecdote, I came to realize and appreciate this act of contemplation, as it is perhaps
the most useful action we can take if our goal is to be a
good person and lead a happy life. Joseph Goldstein was
challenging the audience (and all of us) to ask ourselves the
question: do our thoughts, verbal responses, and actions
make the situation we're dealing with better or worse? Does
our response de-escalate or intensify an argument? Will it
make someone feel better or worse? Will it likely lead to a
positive or negative outcome?

Remember back a few chapters when I discussed my
tendency to worry whether my plane would leave on time?
More than once, I have asked myself, "Is it useful?" in this

exact situation and realized that all the worrying in the world not fix a plane's mechanical problems or clear the skies of inclement weather. The best course of action was to stop worrying and do something productive or enjoyable instead—catch up on emails, browse sports websites, or grab a cold beverage or two.

This is not to say we don't have legitimate concerns in life, such as worrying about a potential layoff, making sure our children are picked up on time, or awaiting the results of a medical test. It's obviously smart to have appropriate concerns about many things in our lives and to make contingency plans as the situation dictates. But worrying for the sake of worrying is *not* useful, and never in itself made the situation any better.

Let's examine another type of situation in which this question "Is it useful?" proves invaluable. Most of us have experienced scenarios where a cordial discussion morphs into an exchange of different opinions and then degenerates into a disagreement with accusation and counter-accusations, exploding into a full-fledged, take-no-prisoners argument. Emotions run high and each person pays little heed to the other's point, but rather searches for a jab or insult to bring the now "opponent" to their knees and "win" the argument. And often over nothing of real consequence.

While I probably over-dramatized things a little in this example, it stills serves the point. Even if not as heated an exchange as the one above, we can still ponder how much better things would have turned out in any argument if one person had paused early in the discussion, before uttering an inflammatory comment, and asked themselves "Is what I am about to say useful?" If what you have to say helps to resolve, solve, or diffuse a disagreement, then it is useful

**Is
it
Useful?**

and should be spoken. If it is only inflammatory, then the answer is no—it is not useful (and, in fact, the exact opposite)—and should not be spoken.

When you glare scornfully at the elderly lady ahead of you at the checkout counter who is seemingly taking forever to figure out how to run her credit card with the new chip feature, and you are about to tell her to hurry it up, ask yourself, will uttering these words be useful? Will it lead to her figuring out more quickly how to run her card, or will it just flummox and embarrass her even more? When your child already feels terrible about knocking that crystal vase onto the floor and shattering it, will further scolding him be useful (will it put the vase back together, or just make him feel even worse)? When your wife is already stressed that she is running late, will it be useful to tell her how frustrated you are that she's late? Will she get ready any faster than she humanly can, or will it just make her more stressed than she already is?

TAKE BACK CONTROL OF YOUR MIND

So the next time you begin to worry, grow frustrated or angry at someone, and are about to say (or email, text, or tweet) a potentially hurtful, demeaning, or incendiary comment, mindfully pause and ask yourself: "Is how I am reacting, or what I am about to do, useful or not useful?"

CHAPTER 19

THE ME METER

S ince the dawn of man, there has been an evolutionary impetus for individuals to focus on the ME,
since those who ate enough food, drank enough flu-
ids, staked out the best cave, and survived were the ones
who propagated and passed on their genes to future gen-
erations. Although we now live in societies where there is
generally sufficient food and shelter for us to survive, this
ME gene, or the primitive Pleistocene-era ME submind, is
still embedded in our DNA and our thoughts. It's ready to
assert itself at any and every opportunity. And in our modern culture, this focus on the ME can all too easily become
extreme, and even dysfunctional, maladaptive, and ultimately self-defeating.

Do we really need to keep every last dollar bill we have,
even at the expense of a desperate, hungry homeless person
on the street who is trying to get something— anything—
to eat? Do we really have to veg out and binge watch for
hours at the expense of spending a little quality time with
our spouse, children, and pets? Do we really need to get
our way every time when we insist on going to the nearest

sports bar for a bite, at the expense of taking our partner to someplace she wants to go? Our ME submind can rage unchecked and out of control, taking over our thoughts, desires, and actions.

This ME mentality is fueled further by ME-centric social media—Facebook, Twitter, Instagram, and YouTube (which is really ME-Tube).

A healthy way to check your focus on the ME is to use the *ME meter.* Visualize an old-fashioned weight scale with a face from zero to ten, and a moving hand (like the second hand of a watch) that jumps from a baseline of zero up to a number between one and ten. Do this when you start to focus too much on ME, particularly when it is at the expense or neglect of others.

For example, one Sunday morning I was discussing with my wife the errands I needed to do. I was trying to minimize my time running these errands, so I could preserve a few hours of the remaining weekend for "Glenn time," relaxing outside or reading a book. She gently mentioned there were a couple house-related errands that she wanted to do as well. My ME submind immediately kicked into overdrive, trying to preserve and sequester as much

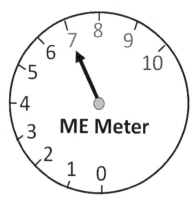

"Glenn time" as possible and avoid running those errands with her. A little later than ideally, my ME meter went off, and I pictured the dial point at seven on a zero to ten scale. Then, and only then, did I catch myself and realize how Glenn-centric I was being. Lydia had things she wanted and needed to do too. The Glenn solar system, of which I am at the center, is not the only solar system in the universe. So I paused to remind myself that her errands, such as some food shopping, were for both of us (as well as our beloved dogs!).

The ME meter can help us recognize when we are being too self-centered, particularly when it is to the detriment of others. But the ME meter, while a useful concept, is like most things: it's easier said than done, particularly when one tries to use it in real-time. The key, of course, is . . .wait for it . . .wait for it . . . *mindfulness*. We have to recognize what is going on in the moment, not hours later. We have to recognize that our ME submind is screaming out to go DEFCOM 1 (all out nuclear war), to protect at all expense *MY* time, *MY* wishes, *MY* pleasure. Of course, in the heat of the moment, this is sometimes challenging to do. Nevertheless, by trying to visualize a ME meter in our minds as soon as we become cognizant of a situation in which we have a choice between ourselves and someone else, we can begin to see with greater clarity the most skillful way to navigate a situation.

Now this is not to say we should become like Mother Theresa and give up all our ME time. That would obviously be taking the concept to an extreme and is a nonstarter for all but a very few of God's chosen ones. The solution to this metaphorical concept of a ME meter is to modify it a pinch. Our mental ME meter still has on the right side of it

ME. But on the left side it now has him, her, or them. This could be your partner, your family, your friend, or a total stranger. We can visualize, in any situation, not only when the meter is swinging too far toward ourselves (ME), but also if perhaps we are being too selfless and have swung the meter too far to the left.

Now some of the wisest and happiest people I know, and whose books I have read, will argue we should always strive to swing the meter to the left—away from ourselves. They recount stories of how much happier they are when they give up focusing on me, me, me and instead devote some of their time to volunteer work, such as helping the homeless, feeding the hungry, or assisting at a pet adoption center. I'm fully on board with this but also recognize that in the real world, we are all going to put some focus on the ME.

In Buddhist philosophy, there is a key concept called *the middle way*. In simplest terms, it teaches that neither extreme of a spectrum is healthy, and that the best and most skillful path is always someplace between these extremes. For example, neither starving oneself nor constant gluttony is healthy, but rather eating a balanced, moderate diet is best.

We can apply the concept of the middle way to our own ME meter as well. We can visualize that we do not want to swing the dial all the way to the left (counterclockwise), giving up *all* our free time or desires, nor all the way to the right (clockwise), focusing on just the ME. The middle way, in the case of my Sunday errands, was to run two of my errands and two of my wife's, with each of us giving in a little, so the ME meter pointed someplace between either extreme.

The ME meter is another way we can recognize when our hedonistic, egocentric, and ME subminds are trying to take control. It's a useful way to help us recognize when this is happening so we can take back control of our mind— our thoughts, words, and actions. You may want to think about the areas of your life where you may need or want to adjust your ME meter.

CHAPTER 20

RESPOND
RATHER THAN REACT

How many times have you instantaneously reacted to what someone just said or did, and as you blurt out your words you realize—too late—that what you said is sure to sadden, demean, annoy, antagonize, or anger the person you are speaking to or someone within earshot? And in the process, wind up making yourself look petty, foolish, ignorant, uncaring, or intolerant.

Though we think we are always consciously analyzing the consequences of what we say, this is not so. More often than not, we voice the first thoughts or reactions we have to another person's words or actions. We *react*, rather than thoughtfully *respond*. We let our ego submind, our anger submind, our self-righteousness submind, our machismo submind, and/or our ME submind immediately take over our thoughts, and we blurt out whatever that submind chooses to say.

How many times do we later regret what we've said? How many times do we realize that what we said was hurtful or only served to escalate a disagreement into an argument? How many times do we wish we would have said something different, said it in a different manner, or not said anything at all? We need to remind and condition ourselves to *respond,* rather than *react.*

On my desk, I have framed a little printout to remind myself that when I am speaking with people in person, over the phone, or during a web conference, to do distinctly three things:

1. *Listen*
2. *Think*
3. *Speak*

The second step is key: to pause and think *before* responding rather than allow my primitive subminds and emotions to react. Listening and then pausing to think before you respond is—you guessed it—a form of mindfulness. Mindfulness allows us to sever the primitive connection in our brains that causes us to react instantaneously to things, words, and circumstances, before we have had a chance to truly listen to what another is saying or to understand the circumstances of the situation. It allows us to ponder what is happening and how we can best act or reply. It serves as a circuit breaker in cases in which our first instinctual response may be too strong, too confrontational, too

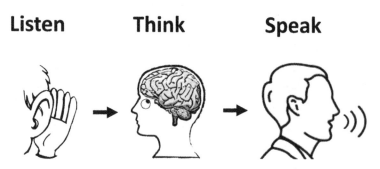

Listen　　　**Think**　　　**Speak**

inflammatory, or just plain wrong. It helps us avoid blurting out something that in retrospect we realize is insensitive, offensive, or hurtful. It enables us to respond, rather than react.

An approach along these lines, advocated for centuries, if not millennia, are the *Three Gates*. Imagine that whatever you are considering saying, or the words you choose to respond to a situation, must first pass through three gates before they exit your mouth. The three gates are questions to ask yourself:

1. *Is it true?*
2. *Is it necessary?*
3. *Is it kind?*

The origin of this approach is a matter of debate, but has been advocated or voiced in some manner by Quakers (as the "three sieves"), Christians (as the "three gates of gold"), Buddhists, and many others, though it is often traced back to Rumi, a Persian poet and Sufi master who

lived almost a millennium ago. Whatever its origins, the three gates approach forces us to pause and think before we respond. If these are too many steps for you to remember, then how about just pausing before responding and ask yourself, as discussed earlier, *Is what I have to say useful?* If your response is only going to upset, demoralize, sadden, or antagonize the person you are speaking to, or escalate (instead of de-escalate) a disagreement or argument, then the answer is no, and perhaps a different response or no response is better than whatever you are initially thinking of saying.

To paraphrase from James 1:19-20:

> *Let every man be quick to hear,*
> *but slow to speak.*

Life is not a TV game show. The winners in the game of life are not those who can react first; it is those who can respond best.

What we learn from mindfulness and from meditation is to be able to monitor or check in with our thoughts and emotions. It is helpful, when we hear something that has the potential to elicit a negative emotion in us, to observe or notice—before responding—if what someone just said has triggered our frustration or anger submind. If we observe ourselves feeling frustrated or angry, then that is a flashing red light signaling we must be careful not to react unskillfully to what that person has said but instead pause and be mindful of how we respond.

When we react, we allow our primitive Pleistocene-era subminds to control how we handle the situation. But when we respond, we thoughtfully pause, using our thinking brain, to ponder and process how to proceed skillfully. In this way, we take back control of our minds. We—not our subminds—decide what to say or do.

CHAPTER 21

SUFFERING

Throughout this book we have mentioned the word *suffering* numerous times. It is useful to consider this concept in more detail and how our minds deal with suffering when it occurs. In an ancient Indian language there exists the word *dukkha*, which is commonly translated into English as suffering. Suffering in this sense refers not only to pain itself, but any undesirable or unsatisfactory mental state, including sadness, discontent, frustration, anxiety, or distress. It is in this sense of the word that we speak of suffering.

As we discussed earlier, one source of suffering is craving, the insatiable desire by our hedonistic and envious subminds for evermore things and conditions (e.g., a better car, a bigger house) to be different than they are. Suffering can also result from the equally unattainable desire to be free from all things at all times that are perceived by one to be unpleasant (referred to as aversion).

According to Wikipedia, dukkha is a derivation from Aryan terminology for an axle hole, which is not in the center of the wheel and thus leads to a bumpy, uncomfortable ride. What better way to describe life itself than an occasional bumpy, uncomfortable ride. Problems, frustrations, disappointments, disagreements, and even arguments are an inevitable part of life. Life is not a fairytale. Life is not fair. Life just happens. That is the trade-off we pay for being alive and living in this world.

Do you know anyone who has not had to deal with the problems of life—from family illnesses, divorce, professional disappointments, financial challenges, and even traffic jams, flat tires, and poor grades? No, of course not! And neither you nor I are any different or special.

There is a famous Buddhist tale about a woman who had just lost her baby. She is inconsolable and goes to the Buddha, asking him to relieve her suffering. He tells her that if she goes into town and obtains white mustard seeds from a family where no one has died, he will cure her. The grieving woman goes from house to house but can find no house in which a family member has not died. After searching the entire town without any success, she realizes that all people suffer loss, and she finds some solace in this insight. Although this is an extreme example of how to understand suffering, its point is clear: you and I are not the only ones who will experience sadness and tragedy in our lives. We all do, and we all will.

We all have to deal with suffering, and we need to accept the fact, like it or not, that these speedbumps and tire blowouts of life will continue to happen until the day we die. Difficulties, disappointments, and challenges in life will arise. It's not a matter of if, it's a matter of when. As Dr. Lynn Rossy, a health psychologist, has counseled:

> *It is not your birthright*
> *to have only pleasant experiences.*

Suffering has been around since Adam and Eve, and we are going to have to deal with it, just like every other human being who has walked this earth. Unless we are able to reach a state of total enlightenment in which we no longer have any cravings or aversions, we will have to deal with the events in life that can—if we let them—cause suffering.

As we have discussed throughout this book, it is how we deal with such occurrences that determine their effects, or lack thereof, upon us. We can accept that these events are an inevitable part of our existence, recognize when one of the many "waves" of life has hit us, and not throw a fit or temper tantrum whenever they occur. As the Dalai Lama advises:

> *If your basic outlook accepts that suf-*
> *fering is a natural part of your exis-*
> *tence, this will undoubtedly make you*
> *more tolerant towards the adversities*
> *of life.*

For some events, such as banging our toe or getting hit in the head by an errantly thrown ball, we can adopt the mindset, as mentioned previously:

> *Pain is inevitable,*
> *suffering is optional.*

We can also recognize that it is, ultimately, our emotional reaction to events that cause suffering, not the event itself. The Tibetan monk Khenchen Palden Sherab Rinpoche noted:

> *We may think that there are various things and people in the world that cause our suffering, but this is not so . . . Everything we experience, whether pleasant or unpleasant, is the result of causes and conditions related to our state of mind.*

The acts of people and events of life may objectively cause pain, hardship, adversity, and illness, but it is our emotional reaction to these people and events that cause us the subjective emotion of suffering. We know there will be events in our life that cause pain. But we do not have to compound this pain with additional suffering by perseverating or fixating on it.

We can also recognize that not everyone acts as skillfully as we perceive; not all of our plans will come to fruition; and sometimes life doesn't go the way we want or expect it to go. As lay minister Noah Rasheta observes

We get frustrated when the world doesn't behave the way we expect it to or the way we think it should, and that causes us to react. We want life to confirm to our expectations and we experience suffering when it doesn't.

When suffering does occur, we can at least modify the amount of suffering we experience. The Dalai Lama has written that we often add to our suffering by being overly sensitive to things and events, overreacting to minor issues and taking things too personally. We take the proverbial mole hills and turn them into mountains. We take a speed-bump in the road of life and act like we have just had an all-hands-on-deck major tire blowout while speeding down the highway.

By mindfully recognizing when an event has occurred that is starting to cause suffering, we are able to recognize it as only an emotion, or an emotional response, to something. We can pause to put the event in perspective and recognize that our subminds are revving up to increase our perceived annoyance, irritation, misery, and anger. We can recognize that we don't need to increase our suffering. We do not need to shoot ourselves with the "second arrow."

Finally, if all else fails, for many things we can mitigate our frustration, disappointment, or suffering by putting things in perspective. If the dishwasher breaks down, the car gets a flat tire, or we don't get that end-of-year bonus we expected, we can tell ourselves that these, at least, are "first world problems." Despite all its problems, inequities, and challenges, those of us who live in twenty-first century America, Canada, Western Europe, and many other places in the world, generally live in the wealthiest, healthiest countries. We are fortunate not to live in an impoverished third world country where many are without running and potable water, subsistence food to eat, or a place to live. The dishwasher breaking is not thousands of people being wiped out in minutes by a tsunami, hundreds of thousands dying of famine, or millions dying of infection for lack of basic healthcare. It is not entire communities, cultures, and civilizations being displaced and becoming homeless due to pointless and endless war and genocide. These are real problems and should put our first world problems in perspective.

As an exercise, ponder or meditate on a recent event that triggered some sort of suffering within you. Contemplate how you reacted, and how you wish you would have reacted. Was the amount of suffering you experienced proportionate to the event, or was it out of proportion? Was this a life-shaking event or more of a first world problem? Did you really have to suffer, or could you have accepted this event as an inevitable part of life, put it in perspective, and laughed it off? When the incident occurred, were you able to let it go, or did you keep shooting yourself with a second, third, or even fourth arrow? Were you in control of your response or were your subminds?

CHAPTER 22

TAMING A WILD HORSE

There is a famous ancient story about a man and a horse that goes like this: villagers see, in the distance, a man on a horse approaching at great speed. The man and the horse blaze through the village, veering left, then right, then left again. As the man and horse approach, one villager yells out "Where are you going at such great speed?" The man on the horse yells back "I don't know, ask the horse."

The analogy may be clear to you. The horse represents your mind and your subminds, which are taking control of you and your life and leading you wherever it and they—not you—happen to go. Your mind and submind are untamed and out of control. You are not controlling your mind. Your mind and subminds are controlling you.

We need to recognize that our minds can be like an untamed wild horse, repeatedly zapped into a frenzy by the electrical cattle prods that are our worry, craving, ego, insecurity, machismo and other subminds. In order to take back control of our minds, and our lives, we need to be able to recognize this and learn to tame the wild horse that is our mind.

As we have discussed, we must recognize and acknowledge that much of the time we are not in control of our minds; our minds are in control of us, and our minds have been hijacked by our subminds.

We need to notice when our mind, driven by our ego, anger, or craving subminds, starts to buck and run wild. Dr. Richard Carlson calls this episode a "thought attack," and we need to be able to recognize when our tranquility and happiness is being compromised by such thought attacks. This is where practicing to observe our mind during meditation and incorporating mindfulness into our daily lives come in: learning to be aware of what our mind is thinking and doing; recognizing the feelings and emotions we are experiencing in real time; and developing our metacognitive introspective awareness.

When we recognize that our mind is beginning to buck and run wild, we can start to tame it, calm it, and get it back under control. We can investigate what set it off. We can strive to respond, instead of react. We can dispassionately assess if our response is proportional to whatever thought or event has set it off or is out of proportion to the concern, memory, interaction, or event.

I find this wild horse analogy very helpful, both in my meditative practice and in my real-world life. I literally visualize my mind as a wild stallion on the prairie, in proximity to a round corral. My goal, both during meditation and in life, is to calm the horse and have it be in a serene state of peace and tranquility within the corral. Often, such as at the beginning of a meditation session, or at the time of a stressor at work or at home, I will "see" that the horse is busting out of the corral, agitated and bucking. Recognizing this is very helpful, as I have now taken the first step in calming and taking back control of my mind. Similar to how one might calm an agitated horse or other animal, I can now try to calm my mind. Gentle, calm, and slow breaths in and out. Metaphysical "petting" of the horse. A calm voice and attitude. Within a few minutes, I can literally see (or visualize) the horse calming down.

Can you visualize the wild horse in your mind? Can you recognize what practices work, or might work, for you in calming and taming this wild horse? If you can, this is an important step in taking back control of your mind.

CHAPTER 23

OKAY

I n a previous chapter we discussed that the most useful three words to taking back control of your mind,
emotions, and reactions, are *let it go*. If that approach
doesn't resonate with you, let me suggest a single word to
help you calmly and mindfully respond to the many situations and challenges of everyday life. That one word is

Okay

I spent the first four decades of my life as a bachelor, living by myself and doing what I wanted, when I wanted,
and where I wanted. When my wife-to-be moved in with
me, it was an adjustment at first, and I was not always the
most skillful at dealing with this new change. Over time,
as I came to better understand my mind and strived to be
a better person, it dawned on me that rather than let my
subminds dictate my response to even the most trivial of
things, I could take control of my mind, and my responses,
and simply reply "okay" to most things. I didn't need to
weigh each decision and answer as if the fate of the world

depended upon it. I didn't have to worry about how this would affect ME. I could just say "okay" and move on. For example, if my wife

- hopes just once to go out for nice Italian food instead of yet again to the dive bar with the finger food I like so much? *Okay.*
- asks to replace the rigor mortis, stiff leather couch I've had and treasured with a more comfortable plush one? *Okay.*
- prefers a colorful flowering bed in the backyard that attracts butterflies instead of the uniformly green tropical palms that I've liked all my life? *Okay.*

Saying "okay" is not caving; it is not being a wuss. Rather, it is the skillful realization that in the bigger scheme of life, these little requests really do not matter. It demonstrates a greater degree of equanimity—that I do not have to react to, and judge, every little thing but can simply respond with acceptance. This is a greater appreciation of the fact

that everyone—my wife included—has their own equally important preferences and feelings. It is realizing that your ME submind sometimes needs to take a chill pill, and that your ME meter does not always have to be at a ten on the ME scale of life.

As with letting things go, saying "okay" is also not being passive. It is you actively taking control of your mind and asserting yourself over your reactive, egotistical, hedonistic, self-centered subminds. It is you mindfully pausing to consider the situation, request, desire, and happiness of someone else, and then thoughtfully *responding* instead of *reacting*. It is you first checking your ME meter to see if you are being too self-centered before reacting, saying "no" or getting frustrated or upset. It is you reminding yourself that other people, too, have the desire and right to be happy.

A definition of *okay* includes " . . . words used to express acceptance." We don't have to contemplate, consider, mull, question, or resist every single thing in life. For some things, we can simply accept them, accede to them, do them, and then move on.

An approach to life espoused in Taoism can be paraphrased as

> *Flow through life,*
> *Rather than try to swim upstream.*

We don't have to let our subminds resist every little thing in life that they may not like or want to do. We don't have to constantly swim upstream or against the grain. For big ticket items, yes, we need to stand up for what we believe is right or best. But for many of the smaller decisions in life, rather than blow them up into big issues or disagreements and get bent out of shape, it is often more skillful to simply go with the flow and say "okay."

Saying "okay" every now and then is not a big deal, and after you do, you usually feel quite good about yourself, and a heck of a lot happier than if you instead surrendered to your self-centered and negative subminds. Saying "okay" is taking back control of your mind and in the process making your life, and the life of your partner or family members, a little bit happier.

So the next time your partner wants to go out for Italian food instead of the dive bar finger food you crave, try saying "okay." The next time your boyfriend wants to wear that out-of-fashion, velvet sweatshirt on your double date, just say "okay." The next time your sister asks to borrow your nice sweater, just say "okay." The next time your mom tells you to bring an umbrella in case it rains, even though you believe it to be unnecessary, humor her and say "okay" and bring the umbrella anyway (like I have learned to do!). Say "okay" and flow through life.

CHAPTER 24

MEDITATION 202

As we discussed in prior chapters, meditation can help us see how we do not control our mind; and how thoughts continue to pop into our mind, as if our subconsciousness were a nonstop popcorn machine and each popped kernel a thought. But meditation can do infinitely more. It can allow us to understand our mind and how we think, and to gradually become better able to recognize and control our thoughts. It can help us turn our minds from an endless series of rapidly and randomly exploding firecrackers into a blissful, single burning candle.

The concept of meditation, though, is confusing to some, and understandably so. There are many different types of meditation. There is *Samatha meditation*, which is focused concentration (or focused attention) on one thing, most commonly the breath (some refer to it as *concentration meditation*). There is *Vedic meditation*, in which one silently repeats a *mantra* (a word or phrase) over and over. There is *mindfulness meditation* (also called *open monitoring meditation*), in which the focus is on being aware of the present moment and the current experience, such as thoughts

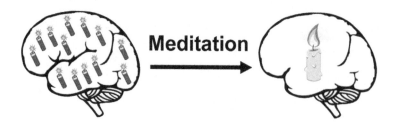

and emotions, and what is happening at that moment in the body and the environment. There is *insight meditation* (*Vipassana*), which involves the open monitoring and clear awareness of sensation and thoughts (somewhat similar to, but not the same, as mindfulness meditation), ultimately allowing one to have better insight into reality. There is *loving-kindness meditation* (*Metta*), in which you earnestly repeat phrases designed to bring acceptance, good will, and love to you, your family, your friends, and total strangers as well. There is *body scan meditation*, in which you systematically from head to toe (or toe to head) focus your attention on sensations in specific parts of your body.

Don't be confused or discouraged by all these types and terminologies, particularly since there is overlap among some of them, and different experts, books, and websites will describe each a little bit differently. Most types of Eastern meditation, with the exception of Vedic (mantra) meditation, generally suggest the novice begin with learning to focus the mind on the breath, which serves to improve concentration and decrease mind wandering, then allowing the meditator to delve into other types of meditation.

For our purposes, beginning with a focus on the breath not only establishes a good foundation for other practices, but allows one to truly grasp just how much our mind wanders, how thoughts "think themselves" (or how our sub-minds push these thoughts into our consciousness), and that while we think we control our mind, for the most part we don't.

The next goal in many meditative practices is to develop mindfulness—to be and stay in the present moment; to become aware of and observe our thoughts, feelings, and emotions (*introspective awareness*); and, later to, in essence, watch our mind think and observe the activity and overall state of one's mind (*metacognitive introspective awareness*).

There is no one mindfulness meditation, and you will find various related names and techniques associated with this concept, including *resting in awareness*, *open awareness*, and *open monitoring meditation*. The technique may involve opening your focus of attention from the breath to sounds, feelings, and sensations; observing your mind's thoughts; or doing a body scan.

Jon Kabat-Zinn has defined mindfulness as ". . . awareness that arises through paying attention, on purpose, in the present moment . . . ", so, in a sense, even focusing on the breath could be considered an exercise in mindfulness meditation.

But let's not get caught up in terminology. For our purposes and especially for the beginner or novice, any type of meditation that focuses your mind on being in the moment and paying attention to what is happening in your body and your surroundings will do the trick. If you get more into it, then you can learn about the nuances, terminology, and categorizations.

I have no qualifications or experience as a meditation instructor. That said, in a book that discusses meditation and mindfulness and emphasizes the importance of recognizing what and how your mind thinks, I will lay out, in very brief and general terms, a few types of non-breath-oriented mindfulness meditations.

In one type of open meditation, instead of focusing on the breath, one focuses on what is happening around you. The analogy is that instead of narrowly focusing your mind's lens, as with following the breath, you open wide the camera lens (or aperture) to your surroundings. Note the different sounds coming to your ears; any scents you smell; a breeze or wind flowing across your body; the temperature and humidity. Do not get fixated on any of these, but simply note and follow them.

In a second type of mindfulness meditation, you observe your mind's thoughts so that you can develop *introspective awareness*. As thoughts and memories pop in and out of your mind, you do not get emotionally involved in them, but dispassionately observe them—how they begin and how they inevitably disappear. You do not try to think about what caused them, or get emotionally or intellectually sucked into them, but simply note them. You may also choose to observe your mind's emotions. Are you feeling happy, sad, anxious, melancholy? What "color" would you give your mood: bright blue, a dreary shade of gray? Is your mind calm or bucking out of control like a wild horse?

A related activity to those above is to monitor and note what your mind is sensing, doing, and thinking. For example, when you hear sounds, note inwardly to yourself *hearing*. It doesn't matter what type of sound it is, or where it comes from, or what it is—just note *hearing*. If you smell something in the air, note to yourself *smelling*. If an itch occurs, or you feel a breeze across your body, or your chest rising as you inhale, note *sensing*. If your mind starts to wander to a past memory, note it as *wandering*. If you start pondering how you are going to fix the broken toilet, you may note *thinking*. You can use whatever terms work best for you. The point is, this exercise again gets you to be aware of and to monitor your mind's thoughts.

To do the body scan, first pay attention to the top of your head or your scalp. What is the sensation there? Is there itching or pain? Does it feel hot or cold? Is there any tingling, tightness, or a pressure-like sensation? You systematically move down to your ears, your shoulders, your chest, and then down to your hands, abdomen, buttocks, legs and toes. You can develop your own specific order top to bottom, or can start at the bottom (toes) and work your way upward.

For all these types of meditation, as with simply following the breath, you can do these with your eyes closed (which is often easier for beginners) or your eyes open, gently gazing downward.

If you are interested in learning more about a mindfulness meditation practice, I strongly suggest you buy a book on the topic, or google online instructional talks (podcasts and YouTube videos) by reputable and recognized experts. The Western "godfather" of Buddhist mindfulness meditation is Joseph Goldstein, one of the founders of the Insight Meditation Society (referred to as IMS). If Joseph Goldstein is the godfather of mindfulness, Jon Kabat-Zinn is the father of a very secular, Westernized form of mindful meditation. The methods and program he developed are now taught not only in the U.S. but throughout the world. He has both books (such as the cleverly titled *Meditation is not what You Think*) and on-line videos available, including some on YouTube. Jack Kornfield is another giant in the field, a cofounder of IMS and founder of its west coast sister institute Spirit Rock (a beautiful place to attend a meditation retreat). You can't go wrong reading, or listening, to anything by these three.

Dan Harris's book *Meditation for Fidgety Skeptics* has numerous short blurbs on different meditations. Pema Chödrön and Lodro Rinzler also have great books on meditation. In addition, there are dozens of other experts and highly qualified, nationally recognized lecturers, instructors, and writers who can get you started. See the appendix for additional suggestions.

Finally, if you really want to plunge in, consider a meditation retreat. Typical retreats are five to eight days but a few are shorter, and hardcore retreats can be one to three months. IMS, located in Massachusetts, is the Grand Ole Opry of meditation retreats. Spirit Rock, located in the beautiful hills of Northern California, is a bit more scenic and spacious than IMS.

The Shambhala Mountain Center is a wide-open meditation community in the mountains of Colorado, and a little more low-key than IMS or Spirit Rock. Multiple other high-quality meditation retreats exist throughout the country. I suggest you select one based on the topics covered at the retreat, its location, and how long it lasts. Be aware that some "hard-core" meditation retreats are silent retreats, in which there is no talking as well as no use of cell phones or computers. This is done to minimize distractions and allow you to fully focus on your meditation, your thoughts, and your insights. While this may sound intimidating to some, I can attest that after getting used to it for a day or so, there is nothing more blissful than being completely "unplugged" for a few days. Some retreats, by design, have fairly spartan living quarters, while at the other extreme some seem (at least from what I've researched on the web) to offer incredible luxury, at, not surprisingly, corresponding prices.

Please do not get too caught up in what specific next step you want or should take. As the sayings go, "the enemy of good is better" and "overanalysis leads to paralysis." Don't research things for months and months on end. And don't keep looking for the perfect meditation technique or perfect book and put off actually doing meditation. Just find something, and then try it a few times. If you decide it is not your cup of tea, then try something a little different.

There is a famous story about when the Buddha was confronted by a skeptic (or, in today's lingo, hater or troll) about this "meditation thing" that he was advocating. The skeptic/hater/troll challenged him to list all the things he had gotten from meditation. The Buddha replied: "What have I gained: nothing. But let me tell you what I have lost: anxiety, insecurity, frustration, depression, anger."

It is true that a meditation practice, along with knowledge and insight garnered from talks, podcasts, and books, will help you shed, or at least decrease or mitigate, many negative emotions. But you will gain many things as well: greater patience and understanding; a calmer demeanor; a more positive outlook and approach to life; a greater degree of happiness; and increased inner peace. And, relevant to what we have been talking about, an enhanced ability to recognize and control your troublesome, mischievous, never-content subminds, and a greater ability to take back control of your mind.

CHAPTER 25

SKILLFUL AND UNSKILLFUL

Throughout this book, I have used the words *skillful* and *unskillful*, usually in the context of speaking, acting, or responding skillfully or unskillfully. Where do these concepts come from, and what the heck do they really mean?

In Buddhism, there is no "good or bad" or "right and wrong." Rather, one's thoughts, speech, and actions are dispassionately categorized as either skillful or unskillful. Acting skillfully involves being mindful. This means considering others' feelings and happiness; considering how other's will react to what you say; and figuring out how to phrase one's words or take such actions as to have a positive effect, improve the situation, or make someone feel better. Sometimes acting skillfully is *not* to say or do something, such as that sarcastic quip you are about to make that might be funny to you, but upon a mindful reflection, could be taken negatively or offensively by the person or persons you are about to speak to.

In the strictest sense, thinking or acting unskillfully is when one's speech, desires, or actions are driven by craving, aversion, or delusion. For example, even though you are trying to drop a few pounds, you impulsively succumb to sucking down that 600-calorie, sugar-laden, chunk of cake (*craving*). Even though you should be studying for that exam, you instead veg out watching season fifty-seven of "The Bachelor" or "The Real Housewives of New Jersey" because you don't like studying (*aversion*). You yell at your spouse because he is a few minutes late for the dinner you prepared, but you do not perceive the situation correctly (*delusion*). The actual reason he's late is not because he stopped at the local watering hole to suck down a few suds, but was instead shopping for an anniversary gift for you.

Acting unskillfully is remarking to a woman you haven't seen in several years that she's packed on the pounds since you last saw her. Acting unskillfully is throwing your dirty socks on the floor instead of walking the ten feet to put them into the hamper, all the while knowing this may disappoint or irk your significant other (I plead guilty as charged!).

I find this simple skillful/unskillful approach incredibly useful and user-friendly. Rather than have an existential, moralistic debate in my mind about something I am about to say or do, it is more helpful to reflect for a moment or two on whether what I am about to say or do is skillful or unskillful. Will my words or actions make someone feel better, help solve a problem in a manner that all parties are satisfied and lead to a positive outcome? Or did I unnecessarily hurt or anger someone, make them feel like they had failed, or escalate emotions during an argument and make a situation worse?

When we act skillfully, such as when what we say or do results in others feeling better or benefiting in some way, we feel happy and proud. But when we act unskillfully, even though we may momentarily feel like "Well, I showed them" or "I put them in their place," upon further reflection we feel remorse or regret. When we act unskillfully, we may make a challenging or suboptimal situation worse and create suffering for ourselves and others.

Controlling our mind, our words, and actions for the better involves a consideration of whether we are acting skillfully or unskillfully. How did you act today? How did you interact with your family members, colleagues, and neighbors? Skillfully or unskillfully?

CHAPTER 26

FRUSTRATION AND ANGER

N othing can displace a feeling of peacefulness from our minds quicker than an interaction that, before we know it, leaves us annoyed, frustrated, or even angered with another person. You are standing in line at the grocery store checkout counter, happy and content. Then BOOM, someone seems to inconsiderately cut in front of you. Your subminds have been "green-lighted" to release negative thoughts or feelings into your consciousness.

We've discussed how to deal with frustration in general throughout the book. But it is useful to briefly address further the common occurrence of frustration and irritation, or worse, the anger and disdain we might feel toward people. Let's examine a few cues and strategies that some notable people use in their day-to-day interactions with others.

The first strategy comes from the Dalai Lama, who describes his approach to thinking about the many people he meets every day:

> *Whenever I meet people I always approach them from the standpoint of the most basic things we have in common. We each have a physical structure, a mind, emotions. We are all born in the same way, and we all die. All of us want happiness, and do not want to suffer.*

This sounds basic, almost simplistic, but pause for a minute and truly contemplate his words. He is saying that we have more in common with others than what makes us different. For the most part, everyone is trying as best they can to live a good and happy life. The many people we encounter and interact with each day are not inanimate soulless beings but are individuals with their own bodies, minds, families, illnesses, problems, and challenges. They, too, are human beings.

The Dalai Lama builds upon this understanding by encouraging us to see things from their perspective, not just our ME perspective. He suggests *"It is extremely helpful to be able to try to put yourself in the other person's place and see how you would react to their situation."* So the next time a mother with a screaming baby and agitated children cuts in front of us at the checkout line, pause a moment and try to see things from her perspective instead of reacting with frustration and indignation. Perhaps she needs to get home as quickly as possible to change the baby's diapers. Perhaps one of the children are overdue for a time-sensitive antibiotic or psychiatric meditation. Perhaps she is so distracted, struggling to keep them all together, she didn't even see you standing in line. How would you act if you were this mother, faced with this situation?

Another approach comes from Ajahn Chah, who suggests we recognize that *"People are not all the same"* and that *"We may want people to be a certain way, but the problem is not them, it is us."* The message here is that as perfect as we think we are, everyone is not us, and it would be unskillful to constantly be applying the loftiest of standards and methods of behavior that we have—or think we have—to every other human on the planet. We cannot apply our standards, morals, and expectations to others, and then get mad or frustrated every time we perceive that they have acted or behaved in a way that doesn't match our standards.

We, or so we think, are always the ones doing things just right. The person on the highway in front of you who's driving too slow is a moron. The person passing you is driving way too fast and is a jerk. Only you, of course, are going the "right" speed, whatever that speed may happen to be.

Don't buy all this? A little too touchy-feely? Then how about an approach I learned from one of my mentors. When someone makes a mistake, acts in an unskillful or seemingly thoughtless manner, or does something just plain stupid, try not to think of them as jerks, morons, or assholes, but as knuckleheads. While knucklehead certainly isn't a term of endearment, it carries a less negative connotation than other ways of characterizing people and their actions. We may not always be able to avoid a negative thought about someone, but at least we can soften it. I also like the term knucklehead better than other pejoratives as it helps depersonalize the situation. People act like a jerk *to* someone. Knuckleheads just go about life oblivious to the unskillful things they do from time to time. They don't *mean* or *intend* to speak or take actions in ways that lead you to react with frustration, indignation, resentment or anger; they're just knuckleheads.

All neighbors gossip, but one day my wife and I heard that a couple who had lived in our neighborhood made some pretty negative and disparaging comments about us. Who knows what they were criticizing or mocking? That we lived together for many years before getting married? That we had dogs instead of kids? That I was a chump for continuing to work for the VA instead of taking a higher paying job in private practice? Who knows? But more importantly, who cares? I am pretty confident that Lydia and I, at least for the most part, are good people. We try to be nice to people. We try to be nice to each other. We try to do good deeds—for both people and animals in need. So I really don't care what others say about us. More importantly though, I don't think these neighbors were bad or malicious people; in fact, we really liked them, and I am sure that if we had needed a favor they would have been right there for us. I just view their gossip, and the negative things they might have said, as acting unskillfully, as them being *knuckleheads*.

As we discussed prior, in Buddhism behavior is characterized as skillful or unskillful, not good or bad. Saying negative things about others behind their backs, demeaning them, mocking them, instead of saying something positive or nothing at all, is unskillful action and speech. It serves no useful or positive purpose and can only result in bad karma. These former neighbors were acting unskillfully and did not understand, as the saying goes, "When you say something negative about someone, it says nothing about them but everything about you." So, instead of becoming frustrated or angry at them, I told myself they did not understand how to act skillfully and thus were acting unskillfully. It's a very useful strategy in life and can prevent your mind from getting knocked off-kilter every time someone says something that hurts your ego or rubs you the wrong way.

I have observed that people more than occasionally, whether intentionally or not, act unskillfully and metaphorically throw what I call "stink bombs" at others, including at me. Criticizing, critiquing, or disparagingly commenting about our looks, our actions, our clothes, our hairstyle, our physique, our weight, our jobs, our financial or social status, our race, our ethnicity, our religion (or lack thereof), our kids, or our politics is all too often par for the course. In ancient times, say ten years ago, it wasn't uncommon for people to say negative things to your face, but now they email or text their stink bombs, post them on Facebook, or tweet them out to thousands, or millions, of people. Their stink bombs are words that can, if you allow yourself to reach out and catch them, cause hurt, insecurity, offense, resentment, or indignation: "Looks like you're developing some gray hairs." "I remember you as a lot thinner." "Your job pays a lot less than mine does." "You're not the sharpest knife in the drawer, are you?" Mindfully recognize the next time someone tries to throw a stink bomb at you. Don't catch it. Instead, let it fall harmlessly to the ground and mentally let it go. As in my situation, I was not about to catch the stink bomb my former neighbors had apparently tossed and let it ruin a perfectly good day.

Finally, remember it is not people, words, actions, or events that make us frustrated or angry, it is our reaction to them that makes it so. As we discussed earlier, we do have a choice as to whether we get frustrated or angry with another person or decide to just let it go. As the Dalai Lama said,

> Anger or hatred is like a fisherman's hook. It's very important for us to ensure that we are not caught by this hook.

We interact with so many people, in so many situations, each day. If we let people's words and actions upset us about the smallest of things, we doom ourselves to an hour, day, or even a lifetime of frustration and misery. We need to view such events in terms of what the Dalai Lama says. We can't jump at the bait. We can't, through our reactions, keep hooking ourselves on another's line. We need to remind ourselves: *don't get caught by the fishhook of anger*. It is, with a little insight and practice, very easy to avoid, but once you are hooked, it can be very difficult to become unhooked.

We can take back control of our mind by truly understanding that people are human beings, not inanimate, soulless blobs of clay, who are trying to live their lives the best they can. Though we are all more alike than not, not everyone will behave as we think they should, and we must accept that. Sometimes, they may have had a different upbringing than ours as well as different norms, beliefs, or customs. Sometimes, their life circumstances have led them to act the way they do. And sometimes, they may just be big ol' knuckleheads. Whatever the reason, just because they act unskillfully does not mean we must react with frustration, indignation, or anger, and catch the stink bomb they've lobbed our way. We are better than that—or at least we *can* be better than that. And we have the insight to recognize that life is dropping another fish line into our lives, and we don't have to take the bait and hook ourselves on the fishhook of anger.

I keep a notebook with a strategy I paraphrased for when I am face-to-face with an unskillful person who is making an unskillful comment or doing an unskillful act. I can't claim, in the heat of the moment, that I pause and remember it every time before I respond, but it is helpful when I am able to do so. I hope it may be helpful to you too:

> *This person is a human being as well.*
> *This person wants to be happy.*
> *Perhaps they're doing the best they*
> *can in their circumstances.*
> *Perhaps they're suffering, or will*
> *suffer, as a result of their unskillful*
> *behavior.*
> *Wish them well in their lives.*

And, if you absolutely need to, modify that last line to

> *Wish that knucklehead well in life.*

CHAPTER 27

IMPERMANENCE

I*mpermanence* is, on one hand, a complex concept important to Eastern (as well as some ancient Greek) philosophies and religions. But for us, impermanence can be thought of as the inevitable, undeniable, unavoidable phenomenon that everything and everyone eventually ages. We decay, wear out, and die. Despite this inarguable fact of life, we often view things to the contrary. We assume our health will continue forever. We assume all our friends and family will be around forever. We take for granted that our pets, while here today, will be here in endless tomorrows. We react with surprise, disappointment, or frustration when our possessions stop working, become damaged, or fall to pieces. We take for granted that everything, and everyone, will remain the same.

While meditating outside recently, I looked around at our three dogs sitting close beside me. Our two adopted golden retrievers are about eight years old and statistically have just a few years to live. One has arthritis and a thyroid condition. The other one recently blew out her knee and only recently recovered. Our small, adopted yak-yak dog has both a rare form of liver disease and a rare blood condition, has come close to dying twice and is living on borrowed time. I reminded myself to appreciate and treasure the time I have with them, each day, and not take for granted that they will be here forever. My mother, who is eighty-two years old, is still in generally good health. But I try to remind myself that at that age, anything can happen at any time, and try to call her, check in with her, and tell her I love her, at least once every week or so.

My dad had a great life, serving as a navy fighter pilot and later traveling the world scuba diving. But in his later years, he had diabetes, heart disease, and pains from a bad neck, and spent most of his time just sitting at home alone (he and mom had separated), not really wanting to do much, and not wanting people to trouble themselves to visit him. Several years ago for Father's Day, my brother and I decided, despite my dad's protestations, to fly out and spend some time with him. Inspired by a Seinfeld episode

about who was the best father, we even bought him a "#1 Dad" hat and T-shirt. We all had a great time together, and we even got him to go out to eat for a few meals. Several weeks after our visit, he died suddenly, though not unexpectedly. To this day, I am so happy we decided to make, against his protestations, that road trip and were cognizant of the impermanence of life.

There's a great Harry Chapin song called "Cat's in the Cradle." It is about a father who has a son, but he takes for granted that his son will always be there. The father spends so much time working and doing the chores of life that he never spends time with his son and squanders away those precious years. At the end of the song, the now elderly father calls up his grown son, hoping to spend some time with him now. But the son has his own life and tells the dad he just doesn't have any time right now to spend with him. It is then that the father seemingly understands. Your sons and daughters, though perhaps often rascals, are only going to be under your roof for so long. Impermanence will lead them off to their own lives, as it should. So treasure your time with them now.

I think the point of all this is pretty clear. All our friends, all our parents, all our children, all our loved ones, all our beloved pets, are getting older, getting sicker, becoming more infirmed, and are going to die, or will move away to lead their own lives. We ourselves, who may take our health for granted, are also going to get sick, become infirm, and inevitably die. I see sickness, debilitation, and disease every day in the hospital where I work and in my weekly clinic: heart failure, stroke, diabetes, amputations, cancer, Parkinson's disease, COPD, kidney failure, dementia.

We're all battling time, but Father Time remains unde-feated. Impermanence is omnipresent and inevitable.

And in these crazy times, we have to not only be cog-nizant about predictable impermanence, such as aging and disease, but the unpredictable, unexpected, man-made sudden impermanence due to drive-by shootings, road-rage, drunk drivers, and seemingly endless mass slaugh-ters at schools, places of worship, and outdoor gatherings. Impermanence is not only inevitable, it is also unpredictable.

As I do the final edits to this book, the world is being ravaged by the coronavirus pandemic. Tens of thousands of people, healthy just a week before, are now dying in hospi-tal hallways and makeshift tents. By the time you read this, you no doubt will likely know and have friends and fam-ily who have been infected and, tragically, some who have died. As a health care worker going into the hospital each day, despite all the precautions I may take, I have no idea if I will become exposed and infected, and through some unpredictable process be one of the several percent that die from the infection. Many of my health care colleagues already have been infected, and too many have given their lives while trying to help others. Impermanence has never been clearer to me, and to all of us.

A practice by Buddhist monks is to spend time sitting in a cemetery in order to better appreciate the impermanence of life. While most of us may not want to go to this extreme, it is still a useful way to contemplate the concept of imper-manence, and to then look around you, at least once every day, and appreciate all the loved ones in your life. It is also worthwhile to pause, appreciate, and be thankful for what-ever health you have now, as well as the simple fact that you are alive; for at some point, down the road, this will inevitably no longer be the case.

The concept of impermanence reminds us to appreciate what and who we have in our lives right now. It reminds us to appreciate our health, our friends, and our family. The English novelist W. Somerset Maugham remarked that

> *Nothing in the world is permanent, and we're foolish when we ask any-thing to last, but surely we're still more foolish not to take delight in it while we have it.*

Impermanence also allows us to avoid clinging to things just as they are, since they will inevitably not be so in the future. Clinging is an important and frequent cause of suffering. Stuff breaks. Friends and family move away. Beloved relatives and pets will at some point get sick and pass away. Recognizing and accepting this allows us to brush off some of the smaller problems, frustrations, and unpleasantries of life, and at least help us better cope and deal with some of the more serious things in life.

The wise monk Thich Nhat Hanh observed that

> *It is not impermanence*
> *that makes us suffer.*
> *What makes us suffer*
> *is wanting things to be permanent*
> *when they are not.*

Part of the Japanese approach to life called *wabi-sabi* is defined as "accepting peacefully the natural cycle of growth and decay." Nothing remains the same. Things, like people, change, decay, break, grow old, and cease to exist. We can uselessly bang our heads against the wall when change occurs, or accept it gracefully.

On a lighter note, we can also use the concept of impermanence to laugh off, rather than become frustrated or angry at, the inevitable hiccups in life. When Lydia told me our washing machine had broken down, I just looked at her and jokingly exclaimed "Impermanence!" When my nice new car got dented by someone—"Impermanence!" When I knocked off the counter and broke a fancy serving dish—"Impermanence!" It leads us to view the glass as not just half empty, but already broken. Any time we are able to still use that glass is a bonus. So the next time your kid breaks a nice vase you brought back from China, or your husband spills red wine on your favorite white dress and permanently stains it, or that 4K TV you just bought a year ago stops working, rather than get pissed off and ruin your day, just loudly declare "Impermanence!"

Impermanence is an unstoppable, inevitable, unconquerable part of life. We can use it to better appreciate what and who we have with us in life, right now; to laugh off some of the small road bumps and frustrations that occur as a part of life; and to at least help, even if a little, to accept the inevitable disease and death that will unfortunately, but inevitably, befall our family and loved ones.

CHAPTER 28

BEING A BETTER PERSON

D o you want to be happy? Then how about trying to be a better person. From all that I've heard, learned, observed, read, and experienced, it is often those who strive to be a better person, who are more thoughtful and caring to others, who put the needs and wants of others above theirs, who are the most happy. I suspect Mother Theresa was happier and had a greater sense of inner peace than the Wall Street inside trader, working a hundred hours per week so he doesn't have to settle for a mere C-Class Mercedes, or the pyramid scheme charlatan, trying to suck that last c-note from the retirement fund of blue-collar workers.

John Wesley, the eighteenth-century English theologian, wrote

> *Do all the good you can*
> *by all the means you can*
> *in all the ways you can*
> *in all the places you can*
> *at all the times you can*

to all the people you can
as long as you can.

No one is asking us to give up all materialistic possessions and earthly desires, become a Mother Theresa, and journey to the remotest parts of indigent third world countries. Rather, it may be beneficial to strive to be a *little* better person. It may be useful to ask ourselves the next time we see a homeless person on the street corner, Do I need every last dollar, or can I still manage to scrape through life if I offer this person a few bucks? To ask ourselves if the ME meter always has to be at a ten, or can we take a few minutes, defer on whatever it is we want to do in order to do something for someone else? Can we instead take pleasure in making *others* happy?

Such kindness leads to good karma, sets an example for our children, and increases the chances down the road that others will act in a similar manner, perhaps even to you. Paying it forward doesn't have to only be what you see others do in a movie or on the news. Princess Diana encouraged us to

Carry out a random act of kindness,
with no expectation of reward,
safe in the knowledge
that one day someone
might do the same for you.

As did the ancient Greek dramatist Sophocles a millennia ago, who said

Kindness begets kindness.

188

And remember, as the Dali Lama, Jesus, and numerous other revered spiritual and religious leaders remind us, other people are people too, with their own lives, worries, and goals of happiness. Being a better person is often as simple as recognizing and remembering this fact every now and then.

You may find that even the decision to commit to *try* to be a better person leads to a little greater happiness and inner peace. It has for me.

We can be a better and happier person with greater inner peace, and take back some control of our lives by recognizing that just because our greed, hedonism, avarice, and ME subminds tells us to do or not do something, doesn't mean we have to listen or succumb to their selfish suggestions.

CHAPTER 29

JUDGING

I n Buddhist philosophy, it is recognized that there are only three ways we react to a sensation, thought, person, or situation. We can like, dislike, or feel neutral about that sensation, thought, person, or situation. That's it.

Let's break down this abstract concept into something more relatable—a Chinese restaurant buffet. As you pass down the buffet, you view dozens of potential options to put on your plate. Consciously or subconsciously, you (or your subminds) are making instantaneous judgements about each entree and side dish. The General Tso Chicken you like; the boiled pork you don't like; and that mushy green vegetable medley that you cannot figure out what it is leaves you feeling neutral.

It's the same thing with all the people you encounter. Many, particularly those you don't know and see or meet in passing, you have neutral feelings about. But many of the people you know, including family, colleagues, and neighbors, you either deep down like or dislike.

Now, it is easy to argue that this trichotomy (like, dislike, or feel neutral) is an oversimplification, and that there is a spectrum of feelings. While this is true, the premise still stands. For instance, harking back to the buffet, you may mildly dislike the stir fry tofu and intensely dislike the frogs' legs, but the basic emotional response and judgment is still "dislike."

The point is we, or more specifically our subminds, are *constantly* judging. Just think for a minute how many different things, people, and situations you encounter each day, and how many thoughts you have. For each and every one of them, we are consciously or subconsciously judging: he's ugly; she's pretentious; he's a moron; that tight shirt does NOT flatter him; that child sure is goofy looking; this fast food hamburger sucks.

As we mentioned earlier in the book, Shakespeare famously wrote that *"nothing is good or bad, but thinking makes it so."* And we are constantly thinking, and our envy, jealousy, ego, and other subminds are having a field day constantly judging.

Remember my neighbors' seemingly endless kid birthday parties? Well, before I had even gone over to the latest one (and they happen year after year after year!), I had already judged—even pre-judged—that it would be *boooor-ing*. I never gave it a fighting chance. Perhaps if I had not judged, or pre-judged, all these parties, and just simply accepted their occurrence, I may have had at least a *little* better time (and in all fairness, I probably did have at least an okay time at most of them).

Equanimity is often defined as a calm and balanced mental state. Although the word is commonly used in reference to how one responds, this can also apply to the mental process that must come immediately before responding, which is judging. For example, one first needs to appraise a situation or a person's comment before responding to it. Would it not be better, instead of judging every single thing in our lives, to simply accept them with equanimity? And remember, the oft forgotten part in the definition of mindfulness is that it is not only "awareness of the present moment," but "*non-judgmental* awareness of the present moment."

Now, unless we have spent years in a monastery devoting our lives to achieving non-judgmental awareness and equanimity, are enlightened, or blessed with the soul attributes of Jesus, Gandhi, Nelson Mandela, or Archbishop Desmond Tutu, we probably are not going to get there. And, short of this, we cannot control our mind to the point of not ever judging. But by simply being cognizant of our innate proclivity to judge, we can at least recognize and then mitigate this primitive response to each and every person we meet, and each and every situation we find ourselves in throughout the day. If we cannot truly control our mind's endless judging and reactions to each judgment, we can at least recognize and temper them. So, as the monk Khenchen Palden Sherab Rinpoche suggested, instead of judging everything we see, hear, and think, and every person, situation, and occurrence in our lives, perhaps try to accept things, at least every now and then. And we should cut ourselves some slack. Instead of constantly judging, we can try just "being."

CHAPTER 30

WALKING MEDITATION & MINDFUL WALKING

alking meditation is often the forgotten or neglected sibling of sitting meditation; it's the Jan Brady of meditation for those of you who remember the TV show "The Brady Bunch" or are middle children. To many, it is not as sexy, transcendental, or holistic as the images of classic sitting meditation one sees on magazine covers and websites. Yet meditation instructors will tell you it is just as important and integral to a meditation practice as sitting meditation. Walking meditation is a way to bring mind and body together. It is also, as we will discuss, where "the rubber meets the road" as far as trying to be mindful and in-the-moment in your real-world life.

Similar to sitting meditation, the goal of walking meditation is to stay concentrated, focused, and in the moment, only one follows one's steps instead of the breath. To do classic walking meditation, all you do is the following:

- Find a quiet area where you can safely walk about ten to twenty short steps forward, then turn around and walk that same path in the other direction.
- Walk *slowly*, take small steps, and focus on each step.
- Don't start another step until you have finished moving and planting the foot and leg currently in motion.
- Focus your mind on your walking, step by step.

That's it. You're doing walking meditation!

As with following the breath, there are different techniques or strategies. One may focus on the movement of the leg (and foot), first noting the leg (and foot) on the ground, then the lifting of the leg and the moving forward of the leg, and then the foot implanting on the ground again. One does the same with the other leg, and the pattern repeats itself.

Another technique is to break the process down into three components. First, the heal touches the ground, then the sole of the foot touches the ground, and then the toes touch the ground. Focus on one foot implanting on the ground, then focus on the other foot as it implants on the ground, and so on.

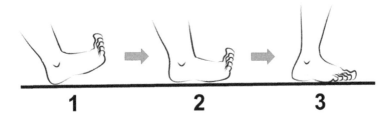

1   **2**   **3**

In walking meditation, you break down into steps something you do instinctively and focus deliberately on each action you are making—the movement of the bones and muscles, the shifting of your weight, and the feel of your foot pressing upon the ground.

Although not considered "classic walking meditation," you may want to try to focus on walking not only when going back and forth on a twenty or so foot-long indoor or outdoor area, but occasionally (when it is safe) during normal activities, such as walking down a hallway at work, going to pick up the mail, or walking the dog.

At the few meditation retreats I've attended, the importance placed on walking meditation becomes clear as about a third of all meditation time is devoted to walking meditation. I'll confess though, that during some of the walking meditation segments of the retreat, I would "cut class" or "play hooky" and instead go for a hike on the many beautiful trails at the meditation retreats. During these hikes, I would still do what is in the spirit of a walking meditation, very mindfully paying attention to each and every step I took. However, once I was able to do this for a while and had established enough control over my mind so it would not wander, I would open my focus (or the aperture of my mind) to the beautiful surroundings, trying to be in the moment and appreciate where I was, but again keeping

my mind grounded in each step I took. I would take mindful notice of my surroundings: the temperature, the wind, the sun shining down upon me, the sounds of nature, the unique shape of individual trees, and the inclines of the hills. Again, I would do this while still trying to stay in the moment and not have my mind wander to past memories or future concerns. What I was doing is mindful walking, a term used by Thich Nhat Hahn.

I mention this story because to me mindful walking is how one can transition one's sitting meditation practice of staying in the moment and being mindful of real life, which is, after all, one of the main goals of all this mindfulness stuff. You don't need to go on retreat or into the woods or mountains to do this. You can practice mindful walking when you are walking down the halls of a hospital, at your office, or in a shopping center. You can practice this while taking your baby for a stroll in the neighborhood or when walking your dogs. You can practice this walking from the parking lot to wherever you are going. You can practice this when taking out the trash.

Thich Nhat Hanh tells us

> *Every path,*
> *every street in the world,*
> *is your walking meditation path.*

With mindful walking, you still ground yourself in paying attention to your steps. But you also broaden your focus to very consciously be aware of where you are and what your surroundings are like. You listen to the sounds around you. You notice what scents are in the air. You feel the temperature, humidity, and breeze. You take a few seconds to truly look at the flowers and trees, the sky and clouds, the sunrise and sunset, and any of the many other things we usually do not notice or pay attention to as we scurry during our busy day from point A to point B.

Mindful walking can be done during almost any daily activity. Even doing this for a minute or so during your busy day is a good way to get into the habit of being in the present, stepping off the spinning wheel or Habitrail of life, and not going through the pre-programmed motions of our often hectic days.

Even if you want to practice this mindful walking during daily activities, it is probably still useful for you to try the more formal ten to twenty paces of back and forth walking meditation first, so you get the hang of it, before "taking it for a spin" in the real world. And, if you do broaden the destination of your mindful walking to a trail, park, or other outdoor venue, please remember, as Jack

Kornfield emphasizes, "This is not a nature walk." It is still an exercise in meditation and mindfulness.

A goal of many meditation practices, and the counsel of many revered meditation and Buddhist masters, is to ultimately be mindful not just for the twenty or so minutes we sit on the cushion meditating, but rather to be mindful *all the time,* from the moment we wake up until the moment we fall asleep. Mindful walking helps us to wake up from our default mode of sleepwalking through our days, and our life, and to be mindful during our encounters with people, events, and situations. The practices of walking meditation and mindful walking are important steps (pun intended) toward this goal.

CHAPTER 31

INNER PEACE

I nner peace sounds great, and is something most everyone wants, but what exactly is it and how does one get it? A quick google search for *inner peace* had 230,000,000 (that's two hundred and thirty *million*) results, including innumerable websites, articles, podcasts, and blogs on the topic. There are dozens of lists of how to find inner peace and what leads to it, as well as a plethora of definitions and innumerable suggestions on how and where to find it.

A reasonable synthesis of the many definitions of inner peace is "a state of psychological or spiritual calm, serenity, and tranquility, despite the potential presence of stressors."

Like many concepts in this book, inner peace is predominantly an Eastern concept, where a greater value is often put on a healthy mind and spiritual health as opposed to our Western, more materialistic priorities. That said, it seems more of us Westerners are waking up to the value of inner peace. In fact, it seems many people value inner peace more than happiness.

I do not claim to have inner peace or anything remotely close it to, but I have had glimpses of it. Occasionally, when my meditation is focused on nothing but the breath itself, and then on nothing at all—no worries, frustrations, cravings about the past, present, or future—I note the feeling in my mind of being perfectly calm. The sea is still, with not even the smallest of ripples. It is an incredibly peaceful and enjoyable state. It is what I think inner peace may be.

As we discussed in the beginning of the book, many believe that a state of inner peace is our natural state, and that it is only our subminds and their anxieties, worries, frustrations, desires, and cravings that perturb our inner peace.

For the purposes of this book, let me paraphrase a few other definitions of inner peace:

- *Emotional self-regulation and the ability to achieve a state of dynamic emotional equilibrium.*
- *A state of calm, serenity, and tranquility of mind that arises due to having no sufferings or mental disturbances such as worry, anxiety, greed, desire, hatred, ill-will, or delusion.*
- *A state of freedom from emotional and mental stress.*

Why are these definitions worth listing? Because these are exactly the things we have discussed in this book. Being able to recognize how our subminds work to subvert our natural state of peace and happiness. Recognizing how our thoughts about the past or imagined future cause us unnecessary worry, anxiety, stress, regret, frustration, exasperation, and anger. Understanding what is truly important in life, and what is really not that important in the grand scheme of things. Comprehending how cravings cause suffering and that most of us already have *enough* for a fulfilling and happy life. Discerning between what we *think* in some ideal future will make us happy, and what we have now that *does* make us happy. Seeing how, with knowledge, skill, and practice, we can take back control of our mind and achieve at least a greater degree of inner peace.

So perhaps the next time we are thinking about the things we want in our lives, we put inner peace higher up on the list than a new iPhone, job title, or boyfriend. And perhaps we then vow to explore the means, be it through meditation, a renewed devotion to religious teachings, a recommitment to our family, a reexamination of our lives, or a vow to try to do more for others to achieve at least a greater degree of inner peace.

CHAPTER 32

TAKE BACK CONTROL
OF YOUR MIND

In this book, we have discussed how our primitive Pleistocene-era subminds will try to fill our mind with envy, insecurity, anxiety, self-doubt, frustration, indignation, anger, regret, and cravings. And how these subminds' desire for more, more, more, and their focus upon me, me, me, can adversely impact our perspectives, our interactions with and responses to friends and loved ones, and our happiness itself. By understanding how our subminds will try to take control of our minds, we can recognize these urges, emotions, feelings, and desires, mitigate them and even snuff them out. We can recognize what they are trying to do to our bliss and tranquility, and not let them disrupt or perturb our natural state of happiness and inner peace.

We have learned that thoughts are just thoughts and emotions just emotions. Whether thoughts think themselves or emanate from our subconscious subminds, they have no matter, no mass, no substance, and no intrinsic power. They are ephemeral and will dissipate into the ether, be it in minutes or hours. We can hold an emotion at arm's length, telling ourselves *there is frustration* or *there is anger*, rather than identifying with the emotion. We can use the **RAIN** or **RAID** steps to de-identify with the emotion. We can remind ourselves that thoughts have no power, except the power we give them.

We can recognize that cravings, such as for that calorie-laden, seven-layer cake, an even bigger flat screen 4K TV, or a flashier car or necklace, can cause our minds discontent and dissatisfaction with our present lives and lead to suffering. When we next have a desire for something, we can pause and ask ourselves, Is this something I need or something I just crave? We can also ask, Do I have enough already, or do I want more than enough?

We have learned that our worry submind can insidiously take control of our minds and that our saber-toothed tiger-era worry submind LOVES to worry. Yet all the worrying in the world will not change the outcome of what happens, and most of the things we worry about never turn out as dire as we think they will nor even come to pass.

Life rarely plays out exactly the way we want it to, and every day waves will hit us and disrupt the calm seas of our minds. There is no stopping these waves; they are the inevitable tradeoff for being alive on this planet. Rather than letting our minds get thrown off-kilter each time one of these waves splashes and soaks us, we can adopt the attitude of "expect the waves, recognize the waves, accept the waves, ride the waves, and then let them pass."

We have recognized that words, things, events, and actions do not in themselves cause stress, frustration, or anger. Rather, it is our *reaction* to them. And that for all such occurrences, we do have a choice as to whether or not we will let such occurrences make us stressed, frustrated, or angry. We can put such incidents in perspective. We can ask ourselves whether what we are about to react to will matter a year from now or on our deathbed? We can mindfully ponder if we want to let this trivial in-the-scheme-of-life incident ruin our dinner, time with the family, or walk with the dog. We can decide to simply *let it go*.

We've discussed the importance of taking back control of our minds so that we don't shoot ourselves with a second, third, or forth arrow whenever something hurtful or undesirable occurs. To not replay again and again troublesome or disheartening events of the past that are now gone and unchangeable. To accept that *pain is inevitable, but suffering is optional.*

We have explored the fact that neighbors, friends, family, and strangers do not always speak or act skillfully, and in fact, sometimes act as knuckleheads. But we don't have to catch the stink bombs they unintentionally (or even intentionally) throw at us.

We have discerned that what actually makes people happy is quite different from what people think they need, in some ill-defined future, to finally be happy. That it is more our *attitude* that determines happiness than our material possessions. That it is quite possible to be happy with what we have in life, right here and right now. And that waiting until the weekend, a vacation, or retirement to be happy is squandering five-sevenths or more of our life away. Happiness is not something we postpone for the future. We should, and must, *live in the now*, and rejoice in the gifts we have—our health, our family, our friends, our life.

We can use our growing powers of mindfulness to pause and then thoughtfully and skillfully *respond* to the speech and actions of others, rather than allow the more primitive parts of our brain to instantaneously *react*, only to later regret our words and deeds. We can remind ourselves: *don't react; respond*. And before we say or do something, we can ask ourselves, Is it useful? We can listen, think, and only then speak. We can try to act skillfully, rather than unskillfully.

Taking back control of your mind takes practice and effort, just like weightlifting to build up muscles or jogging to build up endurance. Start simple. Recognize that late night craving for a snack is your gluttony submind. Tell yourself that you, not your submind, will decide whether or not to munch out. The next time your partner wants to do something not on your top-ten list of things to do, check in with your ME meter before responding, and when you do respond, perhaps just reply "okay." The next time your knucklehead coworker says something unskillful or seemingly offensive, mindfully pause and recognize that your ego submind or machismo submind is revving into overdrive. Observe how emotions such as frustration, resentment, or anger start to build. See if you can skillfully respond—or better yet, not respond—rather than primitively react.

Please do not interpret what I have written in this book to think that I am now in the running for sainthood. Nothing could be further from the truth. I still, every now and then, treat myself to yet another pair of cool cowboy boots, drive a nice car, opt for a nice (but not extravagant) hotel, and allow myself to live a generally upper middle-class life. But I've learned to ask myself if I already have enough. And

I try to remind myself to overcome my judgmental and self-centered subminds and (at least sometimes) hand out five or ten dollars to a homeless person on the street.

I still catch myself replaying unpleasant memories, worrying about missing a plane flight, getting frustrated or upset, and even occasionally losing my temper. But I do it less than I used to and less intensely. I am better at recognizing when I am losing control of my mind, my thoughts, and my emotions; and better understand how to temper and mitigate these negative thoughts and feelings. I still want my "Glenn time," but I'm better at checking in with my ME meter and considering the desires, needs, wishes, and happiness of others. And I'm at least a little better at realizing, accepting, and acknowledging when I have spoken or acted unskillfully and hurtfully, and apologizing for it.

We only get one shot at this life we've been given, and we need to make the most of it. We can work at being happier, being a better person, and achieving a greater degree of inner peace by learning how to take back control of our minds, and with this, take back control of our lives. I would like to leave you with the words of Zen monk and activist for a better humanity, Thich Nhat Hanh:

> *Live deeply*
> *the life that has been given to us,*
> *and help others do the same.*

If this book is of help to you, and you think it may be of help others, please share your thoughts by reviewing the book on Amazon.com or other websites. Thank you.

About the Author

 **DR. GLENN N. LEVINE** is Master Clinician and Professor of Medicine at Baylor College of Medicine in Houston, Texas, and Chief of the Cardiology Section at the Michael E. DeBakey VA Medical Center. Dr. Levine is recognized locally, regionally, nationally, and internationally for his clinical and educational abilities and expertise in cardiovascular disease. He has given on the order of 200 invited talks, presentations, and grand rounds throughout the country and internationally.

Dr. Levine is the recipient of six Baylor College of Medicine Fulbright & Jaworski and Norton Rose Fulbright Faculty Excellence Awards; the prestigious Baylor College of Medicine Master Clinician Lifetime Award; the Baylor College of Medicine Robertson Jr. Presidential Award for Excellence in Education; the American Heart Association Clinical Council's Distinguished Achievement Award; and the American College of Cardiology's Gifted Educator Award.

Dr. Levine has authored or edited a total of thirteen medical textbooks and handbooks, several of which have additionally been published internationally in different languages, including Russian, Lithuanian, Vietnamese, and Spanish. He has authored or co-authored a total of seventy-three book chapters and seventy-eight medical journal articles. He has also written or been featured in several dozen electronic or web-based educational programs, including webinars and audio programs.

Dr. Levine has led and first-authored six American Heart Association Scientific Statements, and chaired or co-chaired multiple national cardiology guidelines and guideline updates. He has also served as chair of the American College of Cardiology/American Heart Association Joint Task Force on Clinical Practice Guidelines, for several years leading and supervising the nation's cardiovascular guidelines.

More recently, he has turned his attention to writing and lecturing on meditation, psychological health, wellness, and the mind-heart-body connection.

Socially, Dr. Levine is a passionate advocate of animal rescue and adoption and the humane treatment of animals, and belongs to and supports over a dozen such advocate and animal rescue organizations. He tries to practice a balanced approach to life, including meditation and mindfulness.

He lives in Texas with his wife, their three rescue dogs, and their ever-growing flock of fostered ducks and ducklings.

ABOUT THE AUTHOR

Photo by Ms. Lydia May

APPENDIX

This list includes many of the books that inspired me during my transformative journey to take up a meditative practice, to investigate my mind, to endeavor to be more mindful, to better understand what happiness and inner peace truly are, and to try to become a better person. I have incorporated the thoughts and words from many of these and other books into this modest little volume. You may want to consider reading one or more of these books yourself.

» *Wherever You Go, There You Are* by Jon Kabat-Zinn. Written by the father of "Western" mindful meditation, this book is considered a must-read classic on meditation and cultivating mindfulness. I recommend you start with this book, but you can also try his other books: *Mindfulness for Beginners: Reclaiming the Present Moment* or *Meditation is Not What You Think*.

» *Meditation for Beginners* by Jack Kornfield. As the title implies, this is an easy-to-read, true introductory, and how to guide to beginning a meditation practice. Jack Kornfield is a giant in the field, being one of the three early pioneers who brought Buddhist meditation to the West, and a founding father of the Insight Meditation Society in Massachusetts and Spirit Rock Meditation Center in California. This is a perfect first book for those interested in beginning a meditation practice.

» *Sit Like a Buddha: A Pocket Guide to Meditation* by Lodro Rinzler. If you are seeking a concise introduction to meditation and want to get it from a "hip" millennial writer, then Rinzler is your man. It was his first book *The Buddha Walks into a Bar . . .* that initially sucked me in to the Eastern (Buddhist) philosophy of how to live life and be a better person. These are two of several books I selected to send to a close relative who was having some problems and whom I thought might benefit from meditation.

» *Buddha's Brain: The Practical Neuroscience of Happiness, Love and Wisdom* by Rick Hanson with Richard Mendius. Science and Buddhist philosophy meet in this wonderful book. If you are interested in the neuroscience behind thoughts, emotions, happiness, meditation, and the mind, this is the book for you.

» *Meditation for Fidgety Skeptics* by Dan Harris and Jeff Warren. While the premise of the book is a chronology of Dan's journey to expand meditation across America, it is filled with meditation exercises and tips on the practice of meditation. You might consider starting with his first book, *10% Happier*, an autobiographical page-turner about his journey into meditation and Buddhist philosophy, and how both helped him overcome stress and become a happier person. If you love dry sarcasm, the book is a gold mine. And the narrative of his experience at a meditation retreat is priceless (but don't get dissuaded by his remarks; most people ultimately relish the experience!)

APPENDIX

» *The Art of Happiness* by His Holiness the Dalai Lama and Howard C. Cutler. If you want to understand happiness; if you want to be happier and be inspired to be a better person; if you want to understand suffering; and if you want to suffer less, then this book is for you. I must emphasize that even though the Dalai Lama is the spiritual leader of Tibetan Buddhism, this is not a religious book. It is completely secular and should will be equally enjoyable, valuable, and inspirational to those of all (or no) religions.

» *How to Meditate: A Practical Guide to Making Friends with Your Mind* by Pema Chödrön. A great introductory book by this beloved Buddhist nun that walks you through your early meditative journey.

» *Mindfulness: A Practical Guide to Awakening* by Joseph Goldstein. It's only fitting that the "godfather" of mindfulness write the "bible" of mindfulness. This is not a beginner's book, but it's great, particularly if you are also interested in Buddhist philosophy. It is long and sometimes pretty dense, but if you get hooked by a few intro books, then definitely tackle this one.

» *Don't Sweat the Small Stuff . . . and it's all small stuff* by Richard Carlson. One hundred short (several paragraphs) chapters on lessons on how not to stress, be in the moment, and deal with life. This is the book that first sent me on my transformative journey. You can read it cover to cover in a few hours or days.

» *The Mind Illuminated: A Complete Meditation Guide Integrating Buddhist Wisdom and Brain Science for Greater Mindfulness* by John Yates, Matthew Immergut, and Jeremy Graves. Perhaps the definitive step-by-step approach to concentration meditation, presented in a very systematic and scientific way by neuroscientist and meditation master John Yates (Culadasa). Not a starter book, but one for those who have begun to meditate, want to better understand how their mind works, and improve their meditation skills.

» *Zen and the Art of Happiness* by Chris Prentiss. A really easy-to-read short book on happiness and maintaining a positive attitude.

» *Shambhala: The Sacred Path of the Warrior* by Chögyam Trungpa. Chögyam Trungpa Rinpoche was a Tibetan Buddhist who later moved to the United States and founded Shambala, a secular form of Buddhist principals, meditation, and how to conduct one's life. While this book does discuss meditation, the main focus is on topics including basic goodness and creating a more caring and enlightened society. It is not a beginner book on meditation or mindfulness, but a "later read" if you are interested in being inspired and motivated to become a better person.

» *Mindfulness: How to Live Well by Paying Attention* by Ed Halliwell. A week-by-week guide to developing a mindfulness practice.

» *Hardwiring Happiness* by Rick Hanson. This is a follow-up to *Buddha's Brain* in which the neuropsychologist explains how we can learn to "hardwire" our brains to focus more on the positive than the negative, and thus achieve a greater degree of happiness in our lives.

» *Loving-Kindness: The Revolutionary Art of Happiness* by Sharon Salzberg. Salzberg is beloved in the meditation and Buddhism community and is one of the triad of early pioneers who brought meditation to the United States and founded IMS. She is the mother queen of loving-kindness meditation. While it is not a true beginner book on meditation or mindfulness, for those interested in loving-kindness meditation, it is the definitive book to read.

» *How to Walk* by Thich Nhat Hanh. More inspirational than instructional, this very short booklet provides inspiration for integrating mindful walking into our everyday lives.

» *When Awareness Becomes Natural. A Guide to Cultivating Mindfulness in Everyday Life* by Sayadaw U Tejaniya. The author is a revered Burmese meditation master, and the book is wonderful but best used more as an intermediate or advanced source of information.

» *Emptiness: A Practical Guide for Meditators* by Guy Armstrong. The definitive book on the important yet extremely abstract Buddhist concept of "emptiness." This book is filled with great pearls, insights, and explanations, however, it is not a beginner book, but rather one for those who are hooked by Buddhist philosophy and want to better understand the concept of emptiness.